Praise for *F*ck the E*

"More often than not we forget we're on a journey of our own choosing. This excellent book gives us a compass for finding joy, meaning, and fulfillment on our own terms."

— Jonas Koffler, New York Times bestselling coauthor of *Hustle: The Power to Charge Your Life with Money, Meaning, and Momentum*

"This book is especially timely in this volatile era where living a healthy, meaningful, and uplifting life by understanding more deeply one's self and thus one's ability to do so makes this book a must-read. I was touched by the specific, actionable insights and examples Ayelet Baron provides to put us on that path."

— Kare Anderson, Emmy-winning journalist, author and TED speaker. Kare's TED talk (over 2.5 million views) on Opportunity Makers TEDx talk on mutuality, also books: *Mutuality Matters* and *Opportunity Makers*.

"In this book, Ayelet Baron offers us powerful life lessons to inspire and guide us. Recommended!"

— Ross Dawson. Futurist, Entrepreneur, and Author

"Have you been trying to shut out that voice in your head telling you it's time to make a change? Sure, it's scary, but isn't it scarier if you don't listen? Can you see yourself staying in the same ol' same ol' forever and really feeling fulfilled in your heart and soul?

Read this book and Ayelet will help you find the answers you've been seeking to live your fullest life. The big secret? It's been right there, within you, all along. Your own curiosity will be the catalyst for the change you know you need."

— Janet Fouts, Founder, Nearly Mindful and Author, *When Life Hits the Fan*

"Ayelet Baron's trilogy of F*ck the Bucket List is truly an empowering read. Ayelet poses questions that are critically important for this time in our evolution and more importantly-for our survival.

Many of us have been so conditioned to giving our power away by yielding it to the status quo that we have lost our individual voices and as a result, compromised our collective future. Ayelet reminds us that we each have a voice and provides the space to explore what that is and to unapologetically use it. A must read!"

— Tammy McCrary, Artist Advocate, Author, and Founder of Artistology

"Written in the language of the heart, *F*ck the Bucket List* is a wake-up call for all who are awakening.

F*ck the Bucket List is a destination you might not have known you were seeking until you arrived here. Ayelet Baron explores the illusions of a failing world and asks us to step into another potential, one rooted in the heart of courage and emerging self-awareness. Reading *F*ck the Bucket List* was like speaking to the best part of myself, the part who truly knows who I am and what is healthy for me."

— Lynnda Pollio, Multi-award-winning Author. Amazon Bestseller in Inspirational Fiction, *Trusting the Currents*.

"After years of conditioning that answers came from external sources, Ayelet's words have guided me to discover what I was looking for was inside myself the entire time. If you are questioning yourself for deeper meaning, *F*ck The Bucket List* is for you.

There are books that give you the answers. This is not one of them. It recognizes that each of us are unique and there is not one answer for everyone. Buckle up, or not, and get ready to explore yourself like never before.

Living life fully can be a very lonely journey. Ayelet metaphorically holds your hand as you take your own steps. What you discover is the connection you find not just within yourself, but with the community you find along the way."

— Tim McDonald, Former Director of Community, The Huffington Post

F*CK THE BUCKET LIST

FOR THE SOUL

Discover the Wonder of You

Book 1

THE UNIVERSE WITH
AYELET BARON

Visit ayeletbaron.com for more information.

Published by Heartpickings

Editing, Design, and Distribution by Bublish, Inc.

Hardback ISBN: 978-1-64704-187-8
Paperback ISBN: 978-1-64704-185-4
eBook ISBN: 978-1-64704-186-1

DEDICATION

This book is for you if ...

You're curious, kind and compassionate.

You address your traumas and wounds
as much as your opportunities.

You trust in the universal process and align to
the frequency of meaningful creation.

You're here to discover the wonder of you and trust
your heart to create the beautiful, harmonious life
you are meant to experience and share.

And, you're so fucking powerful that you're learning
not to let anyone change who you are at the core.

"

Produce your own dream.

If you want to save Peru, go save Peru. It's quite possible to do anything, but not to put it on the leaders and the parking meters. Don't expect [anyone] to come and do it for you. You have to do it yourself.

That's what the great masters have been saying ever since time began. They can point the way, leave signposts and little instructions in various books that are now called holy and worshipped for the cover of the book and not for what it says, but the instructions are all there for all to see, have always been and always will be.

There's nothing new under the sun. All the roads lead to Rome. And people cannot provide it for you. I can't wake you up. You can wake you up. I can't cure you. You can cure you.

John Lennon
singer, songwriter, co-lead vocalist, and rhythm guitarist of the Beatles

OUR ITINERARY

TABLE OF CONTENTS

To be continued . . .

F*ck the Bucket List for the Adventurer: Trekking into the Unknown

F*ck the Bucket List for the Health-Conscious: Trusting Your Heart

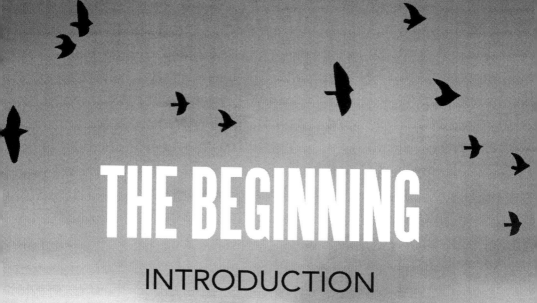

THE BEGINNING

INTRODUCTION

F*ck the Bucket List was created to help you become aware of whether the beliefs, people, and lists that you bring into your life are healthy, or unhealthy, for you. It's dedicated to those of us ready to do the most rewarding work imaginable—asking you to face your fears, your wounds, and become more aware of opportunities around you. It will challenge you to experiment with the vast possibilities of your life, suggesting that each and every one of us has the ability to create a healthy life—despite the deep societal conditioning that tells us otherwise—when you step away from how you *should* live your life, and step into your own power with curiosity, compassion, and courage.

I was told readers usually take fewer than sixty seconds to decide whether or not you will read a book, so I'd like to state up front that this book is not for everyone. It's for anyone ready to start questioning everything, and to simply say fuck it—or whatever words you choose to use when something in life no longer serves you. It will help you become more aware of the choices you make, where you'll truly know yourself and understand your purpose as a living, breathing, healthy creator of your life.

I wrote this series of books because I wish I'd had this guidance when I began my journey in 2012. As author Toni Morrison's wisdom advises us, "If there's a book that you want to read, but it hasn't been written yet, then you must write it." This isn't just another self-help book, spiritual book, or memoir—it's an experience, beyond categories and labels, that asks each of us to tap into the universal wisdom that says we can live our lives our own way. We're facing a timeline split right now, and how we each respond and navigate our life is critical, as many of us are hurting and at the same time being asked to let go of the current programming and build the bridges that are needed. There's no one coming to save us. What we need most right now is to tap into our power and remember that we're powerful creators. Futurist Buckminster Fuller's words are here to remind us that "we are called to be the architects of the future, not its victims."

There is wisdom when you become increasingly aware that this is the era of living in higher levels of awareness and unity, and what and who you choose to consume matters deeply. No one has your answers since they don't know what your questions are, and learning how to ask questions and explore possibilities is part of the way to creating what is possible for yourself, your community, and the planet.

There's another way to address our wounds and fears, and what you'll discover is how you can heal, share, build, and create healthy paradigms like community networks and systems, for example, that serve us. Sometimes the only love that exists is the one we create for ourselves. If you are reading this, you're most likely one of the courageous pioneers our world needs right now. You may be ready to put down your sword because you understand that in the world we're creating there's no reason to war within yourself or with others.

An eye for an eye simply keeps us divided and blind. Martin Luther King Jr.'s energy joins us here: "It really boils down to this: that all life is interrelated. We are all caught in an inescapable network of mutuality, tied into a single garment of destiny ... Whatever affects one directly, affects all indirectly. I can never be what I ought to be until you are what you ought to be. This is the interrelated structure of reality."

A Journey Filled with Lessons and Deep Gratitude

We were born to color with a vivid imagination and live like never before in unity, not conformity or uniformity. Are you ready to discover the wonder of you (Book 1 for the Soul), trek into the unknown (Book 2 for the Adventurer), and trust your heart (Book 3 for the Health-Conscious)?

Life always provides us with opportunities to learn—when we choose to embrace them. I am grateful for the lessons I've learned by facing the challenging people that have shown up on my path. I've come to understand that while people are simply doing their best, some are not for me. I've had many opportunities along the way to learn what and who is healthy for me—and when to simply walk away (and sometimes run) from toxic people and situations.

I am as thankful for the tough times as I am for the openness, generosity, and love that I've received as I continue pursuing my life's work of opening hearts and minds in a world where every living being on the planet matters. I've come to understand that it requires a shift in how we think, how we behave, what we consume, and how we create. It starts with journeying within ourselves, exploring how we can begin living as creators while remembering how to fully connect with others in community—with a vivid imagination, strength of conviction, the curiosity of an adventurer, and the spark of pure, authentic love.

You hold great power and an inner ability to navigate your life. The noise and chaos in the external world continues to increase but the true question is whether you are able to trust yourself and let go of deep seeded fear, sadness, or anger. It's okay to feel into each emotion but freedom comes when you learn to let them pass through you. When you hold on to the past with everything you have, you will experience more of the same. The unknown can be frightening or exhilarating. By breaking through false safety nets and entering uncharted waters, you reclaim your power and freedom. Letting go means making space for your wildest creations.

The wisdom of our elders continues to shine a bright light in our world. In *The Republic*, Plato shared, "The beginning is the most important part of the work." Are you ready to get started?

INITIATION

EMBARKING ON A HEALTHY PATH TAKES GUTS

t's 8:30 a.m. You're rushing to catch your morning train to work. From the moment you woke up, things haven't gone as planned—the yolk from the egg you were wolfing down while rushing out the door dripped on your shirt, the milk for your coffee was sour, and you missed your train when you got delayed in unbelievable traffic. All of these events could lead to starting the day with a negative state of mind, inspiring you to feel as though you should have just stayed in bed since nothing was going "right."

A crappy mood might then influence every moment of your day—unless you choose to shake it. You can bring it along or you can choose to see that the vast majority of things around you are actually working and you've simply hit a few bumps in the road. You may be relieved that you changed out of your egg-stained shirt when you later realize your client was wearing the same exact one. You also ran into an old friend you haven't seen in years when you took the later train, and the world was still intact.

Now, it's six months later and you get up to go to work. But this time, you must stay in your house and not go outdoors. There's a lockdown that prevents you from taking a train and being in traffic. Everything in your life has changed in a flash, as life often will, and you're missing your local coffee shop, getting dressed up, and the hustle and bustle of your "normal" life. You have more work than ever before because everyone is at home and you may now be responsible for your kids' every need, caring for your elders, cleaning the house, and everything else that you need to take on, because there is no one else to do it. But perhaps being indoors will create an opportunity to pause so you can go on a journey inside yourself and question everything.

We would be delusional to imagine life as a never-ending ordeal, but that doesn't mean we should not feel our frustrations and disappointments. This whole notion of being happy and positive all the time is not healthy for anyone, as there are real bumps along the path that are here to teach us how to truly be human. Just like we can become aware of our state of mind and choose to shift it, we can imagine what we want to create in our world and make it real when we begin to become aware of the importance of trust, relationships, and community as the key currencies of our time. We don't have to run away from it all; our opportunity is to face it all with a sprinkle of healthy fear, wonder, and awe.

When we forget that we control the volume of our lives, the noise around us will get out of control. Observe the news programs you're watching, take note of the stories you're listening to and the friends and colleagues you're hanging out with. Do these sources share stories of inspiration? Or are these stories ones of fear and sadness about atrocities and injustices going on in the world?

By consciously changing the channel or selecting different people to befriend, we make a choice regarding what we allow into our lives and surround ourselves with. It doesn't mean we ignore what's happening in the world, but rather that we are opting to live with higher levels of awareness in terms of our own role in the choices we're making, fully aware that the external noise will continue to increase for a while.

Each of us is standing at the intersection of the present moment and future possibilities. We each have our own initiation to life. I would guess that when you were old enough to start asking questions about why you're here and what the meaning of life is, those questions mostly went unanswered—and probably all you were taught was to trust those older than you because they know what's right and wrong, what's good and bad, and how to be successful in life.

You were most likely conditioned to believe that being positive was more appropriate than sharing what was truly going on inside of you. Someone might have told you that to be a responsible human being, you must get to your job on time and your morning routine shouldn't have any glitches. The glitches were your failures on the road of perfection, predictability, and productivity. But did anyone make an effort to understand you and answer your questions? And are you still asking these questions with renewed curiosity?

BOOK YOUR LIFE JOURNEY

We invite you to join the journey, as a leader of your own life, to discover the wonder of you—where life is simply an adventure and work is just a part of it. Enter the gateway of possibilities and leave the manual of how life is *supposed* to be behind, saying "fuck it" as often as you need to.

There are many of us on this journey, each at our own intersection.

It all starts with the conscious decisions we make about our lives—and the most important decision is not buying into the notion that what we do for a living defines who we are. On this path, we're able to sit back and experience the journey as it unfolds, as nature is here to teach us that change is constant and there is never a need to rush.

Change doesn't need to be scary. It can, and often does, bring rich experiences into our lives. Remember that what got you to where you currently are may no longer be useful to you on your journey forward—and don't forget to look out the window during the journey, as you may see something spectacular or scary that you want to experience, or something you are passionate about creating.

What's most important is understanding that humans did not create the earth or the ocean, but we did create the concepts of education, work, employment, retirement, health care, leadership, business, money, justice, fairness, ownership, and success. We set the price of gold and coal. We placed prices on our natural resources from fuel to soil. We've genetically modified our food sources. We've created borders and property lines. And now, we decide whether we work to live or live to work. And maybe there's even a third option that we have yet to imagine about how we could live our lives fully that has nothing to do with employment?

Many of us have been so engaged in the hustle and bustle of pursuing a successful life that we have simply not had the time or energy to be aware of the choices we're making or what we're assigning value to. And we may be exhausted, overwhelmed, burned out, stressed, angry, humiliated, scared, and simply spiraling within the very decaying systems society has created, forgetting that we are capable of creating a healthier alternative for ourselves and each other. We have the power to choose how we invest and engage with life. We get to say yes and usher in what's healthy, and we get to reject what's unhealthy with a "Hell no, thank you!" We have the power to trust our intuition and connect deeply with what's meaningful for us.

When we choose to prioritize a healthy way of life, it's in our power to do just that by reimagining and creating it ourselves. It's far from easy, but we can start trusting the currents of life: swimming upstream and downstream with curiosity and grace. We have to be honest—not just about what we want, but what we are actually prepared to create. Every person who takes action to create a healthier life for ourselves shifts the collective environment. It truly is powerful to know that by changing our own lives, we're contributing to the change of our society—and world—as a whole. Isn't it time to reimagine what is possible?

We're witnessing the breakdown of many of our institutions and systems, and many of us are feeling helpless and lost. How do we take the first step out of the conditioning that has led us to have mentalities of outrage, judgment, fear and criticism of what is happening in the world? A constant need to fight for our lives and survive. But we can become aware and realize that blaming and shaming only creates deeper divides and doesn't serve anybody. Our opportunity is to become increasingly aware of the veil of reality, and begin trusting our guts when something doesn't feel natural or healthy. And there's a lot that is being revealed in this moment, which has always been here, as there's nothing new under the sun.

Many of us have not yet fully awakened to the possibilities and opportunities that surround us. Many of us are still stuck in the programmed belief of fear, ingesting news of doom and gloom broadcast to us from every part of our world, and everything that this fear-based mindset brings to our planet. We may also have experienced our parents fighting or have gone through some trauma early in life, which made us very fearful and shut us down. It created a fear that we must fight for our life and simply survive. This teaches us to go to war every day, trying to solve our problems by applying flimsy Band-Aids to deep wounds, unsure of how to look inward and identify how we got injured in the first place.

We've been taught to suck it up to fight the next battle or live in a delusion of making this world "better." Billions of lives, money, and resources have already been sacrificed to save *this* world and yet the same hatred, fear, anger, and struggle pour through its veins. The fight for our lives keeps us trapped in a divided world (by design), repeating our history over and over. In a winner-takes-all paradigm, no one truly wins for very long.

It is highly unlikely that whatever we resist can simply transform into something peaceful. In a podcast about his groundbreaking book *Winners Take All*, journalist Anand Giridharadas shares that "We talk about doing more good, but we never talk about doing less harm. We talk about giving back, but we never talk about how much these people take and the structures of taking. We talk about changing the world but we never talk about the ways in which they are shoring up the status quo that benefits them and predictably and reliably shuts other people out." When all of our energy is used up fighting, what is left for us to actually birth? Why take sides when we can create something in the world that exemplifies what we envision?

Do you want to spend your precious life fighting, competing, and winning at all costs? If you do, then you are simply not ready for what this book has to offer, and that's perfectly okay. Part of the journey is becoming aware of what is and what is not for you. There's no reason to perpetuate more fighting, judgment, or blame. But if you are here to be the best you can be and are curious to start letting go of what no longer serves you, this is the start of an adventure that will take you where you're ready to go.

AN OPEN INVITATION TO DISCOVER THE WONDER OF YOU

A few years ago, I was driving across San Francisco's San Mateo Bridge to a meeting. I was feeling frustrated. I passed accidents galore and witnessed people cutting each other off in our endless rush to get to the next destination. As I was driving in this insane Silicon Valley traffic, this thought appeared: *I'd love to have a conversation with the architects of humanity to discuss how this world was designed.* Then I started laughing when I realized something so obvious, something that has always been here: in this century, we all can be leaders of our own lives, which is part of what it means to be an architect of humanity.

We've been conditioned to believe that someone else, apart from each of us, is the architect of humanity—as if there is a special council that dictates how our humanity should manifest itself. We've been led to believe that it's always someone else who dictates how life should be experienced. That is the story I had been sold, and which I consciously no longer buy into.

We've been given this precious gift called life to explore the world and create what is meaningful to us, with authenticity and a huge sense of responsibility, as the architect of our own human life. It does not need to be a burden. That is always a choice.

There is no one else apart from each of us that comes together to express our collective humanity. Wars break out, terrorist attacks occur, pandemics are unleashed, injustices prevail, and crime proliferates throughout our cities. This is happening in our world and is created by us. We can sit back and ask for a meeting with the architects of humanity, or we can reflect deeply on the question of what our own role is in this deeply divided world—and then become increasingly aware that when we lead together, with our combined power, humanity can find its deeper unity.

Some have called the questions I ask "deep," but to me, they are foundational. It's not what your parents want for you, or what society wants for you, or what the government wants from you. They don't really know who you are at the core, and until you know what you want for yourself, none of it really matters. So, the deep question to reflect on during this initiation is: What do you want for yourself?

It's Our Time to Awaken Our Ruthless Courage

Through my work and travel, I continue to talk to people from all over the world and listen to what is on their minds and in their hearts. We are at a crossroads right now and have an opportunity to write healthier stories for the emerging world and focus on how we regain our humanity. We can no longer wait.

It's going to take conscious leaders, like serial entrepreneur Magatte Wade, founder and CEO of Skin is Skin, with the ruthless courage to go out there and say, "I'll do it even if my life is on the line. Even if only a few of us succeed, we'll break through. There are millions of people standing behind us waiting for the doors to open. We may not be aware of it, but they are silently watching and waiting. The minute the door opens even a crack, there are people waiting to step in, and eventually that is how the tides will turn." Nikola Tesla, an inventor and pioneer, encouraged us that "the spread of civilization may be likened to a fire; first, a feeble spark, next a flickering flame, then a mighty blaze, ever increasing in speed and power."

And let's also become aware that there are millions of creators who care about humanity and the planet, in every corner of the globe, who are working tirelessly and quietly on transforming ideas into practical actions. It doesn't matter whether it's small or big; every action to usher in a healthy regenerative life system and structure matters. There are many who are tuning deep within, knowing we were made for these times. And we will be seeing more and more people leaving safe, comfortable lives to trek into the unknown over the next few decades.

Transitions and change are not always easy when we don't flow with the natural cycles of life. But when we are stressed out or burned out and living inside mental prisons of anger, shame, or fear, we are shutting ourselves off from the universal wisdom of love and compassion for ourselves. We're being asked to build the bridges between where we are now and what's possible, and we don't have to have all the answers. How could we when we're trekking into the unknown and relearning how to trust our hearts to help us navigate? This is a time of great trust of ourselves and listening to the whispers of our soul.

When we choose to stop and pause, we can actively and passionately start seeing a healthy path where we are fully aware of the source and value of what we consume—be it beliefs, people, food, or services. It's as simple as knowing whether the food we're bringing into our bodies was grown in healthy or toxic soil, and not making choices out of irrational fears—such as not feeling we're good enough—but instead, through a deep trust and love of ourselves. When we choose to listen to our own heartbeat, we cannot only hear our own but also the vibration of other heartbeats around us, vibrating in harmony.

I've somehow crossed paths with a wide variety of people on my journey: Nobel laureates, adventurers who have crossed the Atlantic Ocean on a paddleboard in ninety-three days, scientists who've discovered a new planet in our galaxy, celebrated business leaders, iconic, award-winning movie stars and musicians, activists, and inspiring youth in some of the darkest slums in the world. I've learned firsthand that whatever we choose to create, there is genius within each of us when we awaken to our voice and discover our own gifts. We shouldn't need to compare our success to anyone else's to ignite who we are at our core.

Are you ready to accept that you have the knowledge and wisdom within yourself? It is no longer necessary to attach to something outside yourself to become a leader of your own life. Instead of being a railroad car that is pulled by an engine, you become your own engine, trusting your own operating system. It can truly be up to you to navigate and discover your own path. And when you're fueled with your own curiosity and courage to explore the edges and step out of the mainstream or status quo, you can reach out and connect with anyone in the world.

You never need to be alone—unless you choose to be—despite all the stories our current conditioning tells you in this regard. Paint your canvas with vivid colors, and find the other architects of humanity and conscious leaders who have given ourselves permission to play with pure joy on this abundant and beautiful planet. Open your heart and tap into your imagination, and consider that individual and collective reimagining starts with all of us on an individual level.

Our hope is that *F*ck the Bucket List* will spark healthy conversations and inspire you to adopt a greater understanding and enjoyment of your own amazing journey. What else is there?

This is just the beginning.

The Universe with Ayelet Baron

ABOUT THE COPILOT

My name is Ayelet Baron, and I have had a very successful traditional corporate career. Over the years, I've managed large global teams, and my journey has taken me from global boardrooms in Silicon Valley, London, and Singapore to partnering with conscious leaders like my former Cisco colleague and friend Hital Muraj, who was recognized by Usher's New Look Foundation for Global Youth Leadership in 2011, highlighting her incredible collaborative work across East Africa. My last job at Cisco was as chief strategy and innovation officer at Cisco Canada, where I helped Canada move from being the sixth-largest-revenue country to the second, with two billion dollars in revenue. I held many different roles, which always focused on architecting disruptive strategies that make organizations and leaders extremely successful—often at my own personal expense.

In 2014, I was invited to the Amazon rain forest by my friend Marilyn Nagel to join Lynne Twist—founder of the Soul of Money Institute and cofounder of the Pachamama Alliance—as well as seventeen remarkable women from around the world, including maternal health pioneer Arlene Samen and singer–songwriter Sara Lovell. It was part of the Jungle Mamas program designed to eliminate all preventable deaths in pregnancy and childbirth of Achuar mothers and babies, and to improve community health by empowering Achuar women and communities with the tools they need to be their own agents of change.

Visiting the Amazon rain forest was never on my bucket list. But it allowed me to see firsthand the global impact on the rain forests and the pivotal need for action to help sustain a rapidly diminishing environment. I was struck by the magnitude of how the corporate world had lost its way, and I saw a deep need for healthier leadership to plant its roots in the ancient wisdom around the themes of shared purpose, integration, and holistic well-being.

I realized this trip was asking me to find the courage to discover my own path and say goodbye to a lifestyle I was conditioned to tolerate and embrace, and instead step into my own power to imagine and create a healthier life for myself. A path with greater meaning and purpose, one that might encourage a transformational impact across the world, accompanied by those ready to create on the edges, outside of the chaotic mainstream.

As I started to question everything and make different choices, I learned I could no longer take care of everyone else at my own expense. I had to learn to navigate life on my own by becoming increasingly aware of what was holding me back and taking an honest look at how I was imprisoning myself from living my truth.

I have lived in four countries, so far, and was blessed to work in over one hundred countries throughout my career. Making the move in December of 2016 to live in nature on the sunshine coast of British Columbia reminded me that we are part of nature. It showed me the deep separation most of us have experienced at the expense of unnatural progress and inflated innovation. I realized that there wasn't a universal manual or guide for each of us and that I could no longer live off someone else's manual of success. There was no reason to put things on a bucket list for someday when *every* day mattered.

For years, I found myself lost in someone else's definition of how to live my life—and in secret, I started asking myself whether the craziest thing I had ever done was having a successful career in corporate America as a tech executive. Wasn't it crazy for a rebel like me to have survived in the guts of the business world where I had to give up on who I really was at the core?

I was taught early on that there would always be an expert—whether it was my teacher at school, or my boss at work, or an author of a body of work, or a religious leader—who would know more than me, and that I should trust them unconditionally. There was never a belief or focus on how to trust myself first and listen to the voice that kept whispering to me faintly in my gut that there was another path. I was taught to silence my intuition and put my trust in strangers who apparently had my best interests in mind. And for some reason, when my school bus driver offered me candy and toys for letting him take suggestive photos of me, I refused but told no one until right now. At eight years old, my refusal to continue to take the bus was seen as a rebellion, and I found myself walking through the cold snowy winter streets knowing I had made a healthy decision but not fully aware of why this was better than candy and toys.

I learned about bucket lists, where you put what you truly want to do on a list so someday before you die you can cross it off your list and be fulfilled. I picked up books like *Do What You Love, the Money Will Follow,* and I began learning how to follow my bliss, getting lost in someone else's story. But there was always the hard reality of paying my bills.

Ever since I was a young girl, my dream has always been to write, but there were billions of people with the same dream. The closest I got to this dream was when I auditioned for theatre school and was picked from thousands of others to study at one of the top universities—much to my father's horror. After a year in the program, I found a way to finish my degree in two years, and to do so, I changed my major, to my father's delight. I found myself in uncharted waters, and none of the books, adults, or gurus had any answers for how I could follow my bliss and make a respectable salary. I ended up choosing a more practical route, to survive and be safe. I was told that someday, when I had financial stability, I could live the life I wanted.

The choices I made after the trip to the Amazon were never easy, but rarely is the School of Life easy—and that was an important lesson in itself. I no longer cared about what was easy or hard by someone else's standards. I knew that unless I went on my own journey, I would never know what life was about for *me*. There was no book or person in the world to guide me, no matter how much I looked and sought them out. Too often, the people I brought into my life were not who they said they were, as their actions did not match their words. They had sound philosophies, but at the end of the day we would part ways, because their wisdom lay only in their words. Life was here to teach me and became the most important relationship I could ever have. If I refused to learn from people because I didn't agree with everything they had ever said and done, then I would never learn from anyone.

I continue to walk down many different paths and grow from my trials and errors. I have had to go into my darkness and clean out my own limiting beliefs, from irrational fear to feelings that I am not good enough. I have had to learn to distinguish between what is advertised to be good—be it food, people, thoughts, or beliefs—and what is healthy and unhealthy for me, and how to shift from accepting societal conditioning to living in conscious awareness.

As in any great adventure, there have been some tough times and some amazing times that have taught me and guided me along this path. I've been blessed to speak at numerous corporate Fortune 500 companies and share my experience and knowledge with executives and employees to help inspire transformational change. I was a bit naïve in my passion to not have people fire themselves from their corporate jobs, like I did, but to make work more meaningful and purposeful. I came in with a message that the next big wave is not some human-imagined technology but humanity itself.

I could envision, and wrote a book about, a different world where we worked together with the true purpose of the organization instead of the endless internal battles that take place in offices around the world—during the good times as well as the not-so-good times. I could imagine nonprofits going away because they had met the goal of their cause and had become integrated into communities and were no longer needed, instead of being drawn into the illusion of continued growth.

I shared a vision of a world where conscious leaders lead with a trusted community, and build strong foundations to support why we existed, sparking generations of people who want to feel valued. My speaking engagements at various retail, technology, pharmaceutical, biotech, finance, nonprofit, and public sector gatherings have all drawn the same conclusion: we as individuals are our own amazing app that needs to be downloaded and applied. The next big wave is humanity taking impeccable care of all living beings on this beautiful planet of ours.

What I learned is that it's not about which is the best company, who has the best practices, who has the best life, and who is the most successful—to rinse and repeat their five-step process to success—but rather that it's about encouraging and stimulating independent thinkers. It's about developing conscious creators who adopt critical thinking into constructive strategies, creating our own values and protocols for the collective good. It's not about searching for someone else's "secret sauce." It's about creating our own sauce that works for us because we know our minds and hearts.

This book is not designed to take the place of professional help or a therapist but to complement any outside assistance you're engaging to help you become more aware of what is possible for you to live in a healthier reality, and to be a leader of your life as part of a growing conscious collective on the planet.

The thoughts and beliefs in this book are here to blend with yours so we can become one in our collective purpose of creating a healthier world. I'm blessed to wake up almost every morning with excitement to greet the day. I've crossed many of my invisible barriers and discovered a deeper inner purpose of how I can contribute to creating healthier systems. It's a daily focus and is not easy.

Life is precious and valuable, but is it truly meaningful? Deep meaning can bring a healthy dimension to your life. I'm excited that you are on this journey with me and many others who have closed the manual we were given. This is the beginning of a very important conversation—starting with the one you will have with yourself. Enjoy your ride as you get clearer on why you're here and how to be a healthy creator of your life! You were born for this time in history.

As renowned martial artist Bruce Lee and founder of the martial arts, Jeet Kune Do, wisely advised, "Adapt what is useful, reject what is useless, and add what is specifically your own."

With deep gratitude,

Ayelet with the Universe

EXPEDITION 1

AND THE POINT IS TO LIVE EVERYTHING

The thought of a journey can get our adrenaline rushing. We spend hours researching and reading the reviews of the places we want to see, checking prices, dreaming. There is great excitement in the planning process. But what if *this* is our greatest journey? What if we were to experience life as one big adventurous trek—or better yet, a series of many beautiful excursions and expeditions? It may sound cliché to call life our greatest journey, but what if it is true? What if we were to engage all the preparatory energy and excitement we would normally devote to a holiday and instead use that energy and excitement to explore our own life and our deep, fundamental relationship with it?

We may know how our lives began, but we most definitely don't know how our lives will end. Whether you're longing for more in life, or simply find yourself feeling stuck, I hope this book series sparks your adventurous spirit to explore the vast opportunities at your disposal. I hope it will help you realize what's possible so you can create your own path in a world that constantly tries to mold you into someone else's story.

Just like when you're thinking about destinations, there are a few timelines to consider. The old timeline leads us back to the past, and our most recent collective and individual past is filled with suffering, competition, financial and career success, polarization, blame, judgment, greed, and pain. We've created the physical separation between being safe indoors and venturing outdoors, where we're told it's often dangerous. If we weren't so busy, we'd see the opportunity to become increasingly aware that there is another path waiting for us to trek into the unknown. There is an emerging timeline that offers us bridges to transition to, which include curiosity, self-awareness, compassion, kindness, trust, meaning, play, joy, unity, and cooperation—and a deep connection to nature and her holistic intelligence.

How open are you to rewiring yourself?

Our 24/7 television programming showcases the stories of greed, divisiveness, conflict, need for drama, and violence. Turn on media anywhere in the world and experience the programming of fear-based "news." How many stories are about violence, conflict, murder, domestic abuse, disaster, pandemics, and other fear-generating events? And how many are about harmony, nature, healthy relationships, and amazing events happening in the world? When we scan the current "entertainment" programs available to us, we'll find plenty investigating crimes, murders, psychopaths, sociopaths, serial killers, zombies, violence, and conflict. Then, conversely, there are the unrealistic fairytale stories of what a perfect life should be.

When we limit our consumption of news and entertainment, and their inherent programming, we notice that there are wonderful things present. It doesn't matter who is winning, and what programs are out there, we can choose to see the fear it creates and shift to reimagining what's possible. It's as simple as observing the conversations we have every day—what do we talk about and what do we consume?

When we allow ourselves to be taken over by anger, fear, and outrage, we contribute to the energy dividing our world. And we don't have to stay in this division when we choose to explore whether we can reimagine this world of fear, war, conflict, and division into one where we can create a healthy reality for ourselves and future generations. And as we'll discover here, creation is not just physical, it's about having internal harmony and balance—feeling into our wholeness rather than dividing ourselves based on fear. It requires us to let go of our own wounds and fears, which is not always that easy. One of the first steps is to become aware of what and who may be holding us back, and why.

There's a whole industry that wants us to stay in fear and stress, as it reaps the benefits of us being in an unhealthy state of mind. But we don't need to become the victims of someone else's agenda. Instead, we can become more aware of the fact that we can trust ourselves implicitly, and that the teacher or expert standing at the front of the room doesn't always have our best interests in mind. How could they?

When I had a successful corporate career, I was also exhausted and burned out from working fourteen-hour days and traveling to meetings in different time zones. Every time I felt a physical need to see a doctor, I would walk out with more and more prescriptions with side effects that required even more medications. The first question I was always asked when I called to make an appointment was which pharmacy I preferred. There was already a belief that the appointment would yield a prescription.

It was not until I moved to the United States from Canada that I saw the health care system more as sick care—a thriving business that needed us to be healed from our illnesses through drugs. Before then, I had never had an exchange of money with a medical professional— but from a young age, I had learned that seeing a doctor meant getting medication to address whatever was happening in my body. I also experienced the harmful effects of prescription drugs and tried as much as I could to find healthier alternatives.

In the long term, I had to become my own biggest advocate, as no one really took the time to listen and understand the cause of my dis-ease. Most of the time, I didn't fill these prescriptions unless I came down with something as painful as shingles, where I truly did need to reduce the agonizing physical pain. But all the while, I knew there was another way and slowly learned the impact of the food I consumed, the beliefs I ingested, the work I invested in, and the people I brought into my life.

When I stopped to imagine what a healthier timeline might look like for me, I began to also see the bridges I'd need to take to regain the health of my mind, body, and soul. I wasn't willing to stay stuck in the mindset of merely finding solutions to problems—but when I encountered a problem, I'd also start seeing the opportunities in everything and everyone I encountered. I began to understand that while a partnership may not have gone as I had planned, I didn't need to fix it. There was a reason I made a choice and only later could I see that, yes, the partnership was never supposed to happen, but I was meant to move to the US, for example. And I took full accountability of why partnerships failed instead of staying in a world of blaming someone else for the choices I made. It was far from easy, as it was much simpler to find blame in someone else, but I found it to be a healthier practice, for me, to understand my patterns and how to break through the pain and disappointment.

I started to envision the world I wanted to live in being as beautiful, comforting, and calm as I could imagine it. This world I saw was joyful and fun, and very different from what I was experiencing around me. I started visualizing it in as much detail as I wanted to in my imagination. I even experimented and had children draw the kind of world they would like to live in and compare it to their current timeline. When they did, we openly talked about what they saw as healthy in their life—like when a parent spent quality time with them away from their job, often involving a mindset of play. And what was unhealthy—like kids who bullied them, abuse they experienced, or their parents fighting constantly. Some didn't need to witness wars on television, as from the age of two they had experienced battles taking place inside their own homes within their families. Young children in Nairobi drew a futuristic world where every child would be fed and clothed; even the orphans would always experience love and acceptance.

It was fascinating to hear children talk about what they drew— the stress and fatigue of their elders, the importance of financial wealth and celebrity to be successful in life. I noticed over time that doing these visualizations allowed us to imagine bridges to a world where people live to experience their lives fully. That there are no others to take down, just all of us doing the best we can. I didn't want anyone to have to resign ourselves to being miserable, unhappy, or overwhelmed. With greater awareness of what we can create, we have the ability to take small steps and listen to our own heartbeat instead of being molded into someone else's story.

Some of us have bucket lists filled with experiences that we believe aren't possible to immediately achieve, such as visiting an elephant sanctuary, or attending the Olympics, or seeing the northern lights. But for some, the belief that we need to put our life on hold for some perfect moment when the planets align and allow us to actualize our bucket list, is paralyzing because we carry a sense of failure with it.

We can wait for others to pave our path forward or we can realize that it's time to reimagine how we want to live our lives. If you find comfort in having a bucket list, then you don't need to throw it away. Instead, I encourage you to become aware of why you feel you need it, and whether the items on it are actually yours. Do you really want to go to Peru or skydive, for example, or is it simply something you felt successful people must accomplish? A lot changes when we realize we no longer need to put life on hold for someday when we can do whatever we can't seem to do today.

WHAT WE FOCUS ON, WE BECOME

There are healthy skills we can pack and take with us on this journey that require constant practice—skills like curiosity, imagination, discipline, self-awareness, forgiveness, grief, empathy, retrospection, resilience, honesty, self-respect, experimentation, courage, kindness, and joy (add any others that you feel are healthy). We get to decide what we want to bring along and what we want to leave behind— things like hate, outrage, blame, jealousy, shame, competition, scarcity, anger, fear, and stress, for example.

Much depends on what you value and what you want to develop on your journey to greater health and well-being—both for yourself and for your fellow travelers. All any of us ever wants is to be seen for who we are, but so many of us have lost pieces of ourselves along the way. And now, we're each being asked to face ourselves, at our own pace. How we respond and react is personal. There's no best practice or process to follow when we open ourselves to our life.

When it comes to being human, there isn't a lot that's changed in the fundamental sense; we still face challenges similar to those of the generations before us. Even though we may have more technology available to us than previous generations, if we want to connect deeply with people, what we need is not only to trust ourselves, but to bring curiosity, passion, and imagination of life and the world we want to live in and co-create. It's a time to ask yourself what's working and what's not working in how you're approaching your life, and whether what you're focusing on is truly healthy for you.

Becoming Aware of Your Ability to Reimagine and Create

Living in large modern cities is an experience that's less than 200 years old, and the same is true for business. And yet, many people choose not to question how we got here, and instead blindly accept this reality. We look at the current systems—social, political, health, financial, legal, business, or any other that society has created—and accept them as they are. But, as mentioned earlier, should we not truly understand who truly created them? And why do so many of us believe we can only fix them or make them better, when we can build the bridges we need to create healthier and more intelligent ones as we trek into the unknown?

We have literally come to a point in time where we as human beings accept the current systems as they are without acknowledging that we are the ones who created or inherited them. Granted, humans did not create the sun, the ocean, the sky, the earth, or animals but we did create the notion of work, money, vacations, marriage, retirement, taxes, the stock market, government, and the health care system. The human imagination is immense. And don't forget, we also created the wheel, airplanes, pencils, music, pizza, and the internet—and there is so much more that we can create when we reimagine what is possible. It starts with deep questioning and curiosity to explore what healthy education, health care, financial, political, and societal systems look like when they serve us. And maybe there are systems and an infrastructure that we need that have yet to exist? Maybe that's why you're here?

While it would be impossible to redesign the natural systems—the oceans, the wind currents, the soil, and the planets—it is not insane to believe that we can reimagine existing man-made systems and develop healthy approaches and systems that would create healthier, regenerative, and more personally satisfying options for our world.

Do you remember being asked at a young age what you wanted to do or be when you grew up? How did you answer that question, and at what age? Now imagine—just imagine—that instead of that question, you were asked (and maybe you were!) questions like, "Why do you think you're here? What do you want to create while you're on this planet?" Do you know how you would have answered that question as a young child? How would you answer it right now?

We were born with an ability to examine what is possible and to become aware of our own operating system—our beliefs, our consumption, our attention, our way of life, and the role of work in our life. It's not about blaming or judging, as the only person we can change in our lifetime is ourselves, but rather it's about examining what we are bringing into our world and how we want to show up for ourselves and our communities. There are amazing things happening all over the planet right now, even when things may seem hopeless; you just have to be open to find or create them.

Who Defined Success?

For a big part of my life, I defined myself by what I did for a living—measuring my success and failure by the external metrics that surrounded me every day. The story I was sold was that a solid education with numerous degrees would open many doors. It would allow me to move up the ranks. By outperforming everyone else, I would be on the path to a successful career and life.

Does any of this sound familiar to you? Maybe because it's the narrative of our times. But what no one tells us is that there is a high personal cost to being very successful, and there is a big difference between achieving our personal best and being the best in the world. When we move up the coveted corporate ladder and get exposed to the top of the corporation, for example, we'll most likely be disappointed after the initial euphoria of success. And once we've fought our way to the "top," we've also got to fight to stay there, which is something so few of us ever really consider.

According to Albert Einstein, "the world as we have created it is a process of our thinking. It cannot be changed without changing our thinking." An increasing number of people are starting to redefine what it really means to be successful, and it no longer includes the corporation's insatiable appetite for growth in profits, shareholder value, and productivity, at our own expense. The current global business model, which demands constant growth, productivity, and a parochial version of efficiency, no longer serves the vast majority of humanity—and never really served any of us, in a deeper sense.

Many of us are realizing that we don't need to balance work and life, but simply need to have a meaningful life that is balanced and rich with whatever we choose to invite into it. There's plenty of energy that we all have available to invest in joy and self-fulfillment, provided we have a healthy mindset. There's no one to compare ourselves to, about who's got life right, when we become aware that it's our life to live. We can no longer afford to separate work and life and spend our time trying to balance this divisive myth, which enslaves us to focus on how we make a living and squeeze our lives into non-working time. We don't need more of the same programs or mindsets; that's just rearranging the deck chairs on a sinking ship.

Business itself is at the edge of a major transformation that is slowly unfolding, with more people of all ages wanting to make an impact through our work. Many people are starting to understand we can make different choices about how we want to spend our lives. It's a reminder that we cannot continue on the current trajectory for much longer. While the media endlessly celebrates successful corporations for their profitability, and countries for their gross domestic product (GDP) growth, there is a growing epidemic of busyness, where people are not able to find the time to live our lives fully outside of the confines of our careers and never-ending pursuit of "making a living." In *The Art of Possibility*, author Rosamund Stone Zander shares that "in the measurement world, you set a goal and strive for it. In the universe of possibility, you set the context and let life unfold."

Isn't it a bit insane that the World Health Organization (WHO) declared in 2019 that burnout is a mental health issue? Instead of acknowledging its root cause—which is almost always job-related—the finger of blame is shifted to point at the victims of this common experience. Isn't it time to look deeper at why so many "successful" people are feeling lonely and depressed? Why have we not classified greed as a mental illness that creates burnout? And what about the insatiable need to be productive and efficient? These are metrics of self-worth that have been conditioned into our psyche, especially in North America. In my former workplace, women giving birth and coming back to work after only a week of maternity leave were celebrated as heroes, while my European employees often spent the first year of their child's life nurturing them.

We have created these very systems and metrics, and we continue to feed their insatiable appetites. When we choose to face our darkness and take responsibility for it, we're free to come to terms with the aspects of ourselves that have gone astray, both individually and collectively. Take productivity, for example—it makes us judge ourselves harshly when we don't complete our to-do list for the day or tick items off our bucket lists by the end of our lives. Many of us go to bed every night haunted by the number of emails that remain unanswered in our inbox. But what actually happens when we don't respond to all our emails? And who benefits when we're all super-productive and efficient? Why does it really matter? We've been sold that we have to be productive and spend our time efficiently. No one wants to be called lazy or seen as unproductive. We've been led to believe that we must stuff our days with activities—even meditation, yoga, working out, and self-care have become qualifiers for a successful day. Why do we create a life that we need to vacate or detox from?

In the end, the answer and the questions rest and wrestle within us. There is no one left to point fingers at when we realize that while we may not have personally created these systems, we still have endorsed and fed into them. Our real work is to pay attention to our well-being so that we can support our overall health. We can be productive at work, but not at the expense of our health. We can have a bucket list, but not put our life on hold.

In fact, we may have an opportunity to take a fresh approach and make sure we're motivated by inspiration and grounded in reality. It could be easy to fall prey to illusions and norms, but the antidote lies in not overlooking details or running before we can walk. What acts—small and big—can you put your heart, mind, intellect, and soul into? Where is your curiosity, spontaneity, and joy? What defines your own success? Please take whatever time you need to sit or walk or skip with these questions, and also please add your own questions.

WE HAVE A GIGANTIC OPPORTUNITY
TO REDEFINE OUR LIVES

We no longer know what "work" really means, apart from making a living so we can support the lifestyle we were told would make us happy. Some people work two to three shift jobs to put food on the table and pay their rent, while others never seem to stop working, even on weekends and vacations. And let's not forget the trust fund babies flying around the world in their private jets, whose jobs consist of seeking meaning everywhere they go. The irony is that there are many people predicting the future of work, but we fail to have a shared understanding of what work could mean in this century and how it can benefit people, society, and the planet.

There is also the often horrible and senseless destruction of our environment in the pursuit of maximizing profit at any cost, which is basically like dumping toxic waste into our own living room. We wouldn't put harmful chemicals in the gas tank of an expensive car, so why do we put them in our own bodies? Why do packages now tell us when our food is safe to consume and when it is unsafe and genetically modified? Have we not been consuming fast food that poisons our bodies for the last fifty years, making some people super wealthy as a result, and rendering the rest of us filled with disease and fear? There are people who are becoming increasingly aware of the cracks that are starting to show in how corporations are run, but not many people have any idea how to address them.

When you find yourself contemplating what is right and what is wrong, what is good and what is bad, take a moment to think of who created the framework distinguishing what is right from what is wrong. Someone may provide us with a list of the twenty-one foods that we should never eat because they're bad for us, but do they know our body? And sure, research does help to discover what is good for us, but the more significant question is which foods are healthy for our specific body type? Do we know the source of the food we consume and whether it has been genetically modified or kept pure? It's bigger than just knowing how to keep our body healthy—we've been locked into a program of choosing sides and making right and wrong choices our entire lives. Isn't there always a perceived consequence when we don't choose the right job, the right partner, or the right shoes?

But imagine for a moment that you are alone in the world and you get to choose the life you want to live. You're at a crossroads where you can choose one of several paths. There is no one judging you for the choices you will make and there's no need to defend your choices, either. It's up to you to decide, for yourself, what is healthy and unhealthy for you. Now, take a breath. What opportunity do you see? Which one gets you so excited that you feel an energy surge when you visualize it?

Now imagine that you're no longer alone on the planet; there are other people here with you. What choice would you now make—one that is deemed good by the people around you, or one that you feel is healthy for you? What does it look like when you imagine living to your fullest potential? Can you afford not to go down this path?

When we're constantly needing to defend our positions and worry about the choices we make, we get stuck in our problems. Our energy stagnates and we become more concerned about what others think than what our intuition is signaling to us. It doesn't matter whether our resistance comes from external or internal judgment— the outcome tends to be the same. Fear of judgment or making wrong choices keeps us frozen in our problems. It keeps us stuck between two points, never moving forward to explore what lies beyond the horizon.

With each action you take, you can observe whether you're stuck in the existing paradigm of taking a hammer to every nail, or if you're letting go of structures that no longer serve you to create a life that may be unimaginable to some, especially people stuck in our current paradigms. Can you take a moment to imagine what would happen when you let go of any painful or shameful experience that is holding you in the past? For me, this has become a way to acknowledge my true power. And in an instant, a small shift takes place in how I approach a situation or a person.

When mainstream leaders tell us to fight for our life, or war against something or someone, we simply give energy to fear and anger. When we're in a powerless state, we don't see opportunities. It's never healthy to stay in resistance, which is created from fear and anger. It keeps us warring and divided. When we can start looking for possibilities, our hearts naturally guide us to what is healthy, to our own power source. When we get into a state of flow, we can see these opportunities. What's your state of nonresistance? Have you ever been in flow, focusing on what's possible?

Leadership is not outside ourselves, and there is no authority figure that has the right to govern us to stay in conflict and keep us leading our lives in fear—that is, unless we ourselves give in to unhealthy fear. When we start to question everything, we get in touch with who we are at the core and relearn our right to discover joy and peace in our lives. But if we stay committed to a dying paradigm's belief system that suggests we're only here to solve the same problems, and not create a new way, we will stay stuck in a decaying world constructed from consumption, competition, division, and fear.

There's Abundant Hope When We Adopt an Opportunity Mindset

While this may sound bleak to some, it is actually one of our biggest opportunities to create healthier systems that serve us instead

Information Regarding Increased Premiums Resulting From Accidents

(Please disregard if you have not had an accident or if rated as a commercial vehicle)

you have been involved in an automobile accident
hich resulted in an accident surcharge, the amount
ue indicated on the enclosed statement will show
he increased premium. If any of the conditions
sted below applies to your situation, the surcharge
ay be removed. Pay the amount shown on the
enewal notice and give us the full facts as to why the
rcharge should be removed. We will reimburse you
he difference in premium for any surcharge removed.

he insured vehicle was:

Lawfully parked, or

Struck in the rear by another vehicle headed in the
same direction, and the driver of your vehicle has
not been convicted of a moving traffic violation in
connection with the accident, or

Hit by a "hit-and-run" driver and the accident was
reported to the proper authorities within 24 hours
of discovery, or

(continued on back)

The driver of the insured vehicle:

a. Was reimbursed by, or on behalf of, a person responsible for the accident or has judgment against such person, or

b. Was not convicted of a moving traffic violation in connection with the accident, but the driver of the other automobile involved in such accident was convicted of a moving traffic violation, or

c. Was finally judged not to be liable by a court of competent jurisdiction, or

d. Was issued a traffic citation which was dismissed, or which the prosecutor declined to prosecute, or

e. Was not at fault and provides a written statement establishing facts demonstrating lack of fault, which are not rebutted by information in our files from which we, in good faith, determine that the insured was substantially at fault, or

f. Is no longer a member of your household, or

g. Will not be driving your car in the future, or

h. Was less than 50% at fault.

State Farm Mutual Automobile Insurance Company
State Farm Fire and Casualty Company
Bloomington, IL

of continuing to serve the decaying systems we're keeping on life support. Many people spend their lives trying to rage against the machine, which is honorable, but what if there is another path that invites us to simply band together, break away, and create healthier systems?

We can chart a healthy course for ourselves and for the community. It requires us to pause, reimagine, and rethink our way forward, both as individuals and as organizations—like companies that use natural ingredients instead of animal testing for their cosmetics, or those who have transformed the traditional pet store model by renouncing puppy mill suppliers in favor of shelter dogs. There are people building healthy school systems and regenerative agriculture practices. This time in history is calling each of us to be the architects our world needs. The words of philosopher Rudolf Steiner guide us to understand that "a healthy social life arises when the whole community finds its reflection in the mirror of a person's soul, and when the virtue of each person lives in the whole community."

Most of us would prefer to work at and shop from organizations that have people-centered practices in the basic fabric of how they do business. Putting people first encompasses not only how employees are treated, but how customers, the community, the environment, and even shareholders are engaged with the company. The businesses that truly value people—not as mere consumers, or as liabilities or resources, but as fellow human beings on our shared journey—are more likely to succeed in the long term. And this is where the choices we make every day about what we consume matter deeply.

When we feel genuinely valued, we are more eager to bring our talents and hearts to our work, and that can only benefit everyone, especially our children, elders, and communities—and let's always remember that we tell people how to treat us by the choices we make and how we show up in the world. It's a two-way street when we find the courage to let an organization or an employer know that we value how they treat people and the environment. So, where are the leaders our world needs most? Well, we're right here, and it's up to us to find each other when we are ready. And here is a hint: conscious leaders are not swimming in the mainstream. When we look, we can find each other at the edges quietly building healthy schools, biodynamic farms, circular economies, and other healthy structures for the emerging world.

THE PATH IS WAITING FOR US

It probably won't surprise you that massive change isn't going to come from large organizations or leaders who currently have limited incentive, beyond lip service, to care about people and humanity more than the financial bottom line. When we continue to measure productivity, efficiency, growth, and shareholder value, workers continue to be disposable—and it's partly because many people still show up every day and collect their paycheck every two weeks to pay their bills, and there are always more people around the corner ready to earn their keep. It's just how things are now.

We've given organizations and institutions power over us. We've been trained to fight and fear for our lives, as opposed to feeling empowered to create healthy and fulfilling lives. How does your interaction with any media leave you feeling? And are you aware of what you're consuming? Information isn't harmful, but information that creates a negative state of being will bring you down with it. Just remember that in every moment in time, you have just as much opportunity to create positive things in your life as you do to . perpetuate or accept the negative things holding you back. For some it's planting a garden, while for others it's snuggling with a book that lifts our spirits. By staying in fear and anger, we perpetuate that energy not only in our own lives but in society itself. How can we become fully aware of what we are consuming by making unconscious behaviors conscious?

Change is slowly emerging from people living in higher levels of consciousness and who lead our own lives with pure empathy, generosity, and an opportunity mindset. We don't allow ourselves to enter the stage of programmed fear or anger in challenging situations. We understand that sometimes signing petitions, for example, can keep us stuck in already broken systems that are beyond fixing. Instead of fighting the system, we embrace the opportunity to imagine the world we want to live in, and we create it by tapping into our own power source. There is no one to take down, protest against, or fight when we don't allow anyone to control us. It's important to become aware of our limiting beliefs—which will happen in the upcoming expeditions in this book—and face our individual societal conditioning.

This is precisely why we're entering some very exciting times in human history, which include people like you and me, who are finding our voices and redefining what having a successful life means to us. We're learning to say no and walk away from toxic situations and people. It's not an easy choice to make, but with the state of the world, it's one being asked of each of us more and more.

The societal change we covet starts on an individual level. There's a way to transform the story of suffering and survival into one of creation by seeing opportunities and discovering the wonder of you. You may have picked up this book because you feel a responsibility and yearning to more wisely navigate the future course of your life. As you start to recognize that you have more choices, and that there are many paths you can take on this journey, you can start to reimagine what life means to you and what relationship you want to have with work, beyond making a living.

A great deal changed for me when I started this journey and my dear friend Bill advised me on a rainy day that God has 7.7 billion backup plans (the number of people on the planet at the time). He told me that I didn't have to shoulder the responsibility for all of humanity to live a meaningful life and create healthy realities. My job was to help as many people as I could who are ready to join the journey in remembering how beautiful and powerful we are.

On these pages, you will find pieces of my own journey, as I am not sharing anything that I did not go through myself. I've taken so many risks, walked down some unknown paths, and experienced many heartbreaks, and I would do it all again to be in this state of awareness by learning how to be gentle with myself so I can better reimagine what's possible for us.

Not at Our Own Expense

One of the biggest lessons I have learned is that I no longer do things at my own expense. While I was once taught to "suck it up," I now simply walk away from toxic people and situations because I want to spend my life with healthy people who feed my curiosity and soul. Not only are there 7.7 billion people on this abundant planet, there are also many opportunities that may first appear a bit scary but are equally available to each of us.

I have met youth living in some of the darkest slums on earth who inspired me more deeply with their visions of life than people in the boardrooms I frequented in Silicon Valley, London, Singapore, Tokyo, or Toronto. I realized that each of us has an ability to see the world with healthy eyes, as indigenous people do: a world that is sufficient, filled with intelligence, creativity, and mystery. A world where we stop working so hard to get from point A to B, with goals to achieve, and instead spend our time and energy understanding our place in harmony with nature. Instead of achieving goal after goal, we can journey deeper into ourselves to discover and connect with the wonder within us.

As the decaying institutions on our planet continue to crumble, we can look up and see the storm passing as we feel the sun's rays on our face. Each of us has an infinite capacity to dream, create, collaborate, and make a difference in how we choose to show up in life, when we can reimagine what we need as it is already and has always been here. The African youth taught me that I am enough.

After firing myself from my corporate job, I discovered that my role was later divided among three men who were now responsible for my workload. I learned that as a woman, I was brought up to please others, and friends would often tell me that I was too generous. It confused me because I didn't realize someone could even be too generous. Aren't we either generous or not at all? But as I experienced more of life, I realized that I often made choices at my own expense, and I had to get to the root cause of why I didn't value myself enough to take better care of myself. Slowly, and through many experiences, I learned to set some boundaries. Because when I was out of balance, I could not really help anyone else. I learned that self-love was not narcissism but rather a matter of being self-aware of what and who was healthy for me.

I would often get excited when I'd meet somebody and think we could work together, only later to realize I didn't do enough investigation as to their real agendas, their wounds, and their true ability to partner. It was a pattern for me of getting enthused by people who would say things that resonated with me and believing they were the ones I had been looking to collaborate with, only to find that their actions did not match their words. It can happen to any of us when we find a new job, a new partnership, or a new love.

I learned that just because someone won awards for their work on peace didn't mean they knew how to collaborate with shared purpose. I found by spending time with them and having a front row seat to their lives that they had no peace in their relationships with their children, for example. They were being viewed as the champions of peace, and yet, behind closed doors, I felt their pain and hurt as a parent who had constant internal battles with their kids. I met people who told me beautiful stories, and the more I worked with them, the more I learned these stories were not grounded in reality. I experienced firsthand that what they said did not match how they showed up in the world. I learned it was okay to walk away from seductive and prestigious projects, people, and roles that didn't suit me, even if everybody else thought I was insane.

Over time, my hurt and disappointment lessened because I learned not to do things at my own expense and not to fall in love with someone else's dreams. The healthiest thing I could do was walk away from toxic situations and people when they were unhealthy to my well-being—but what I learned is not to do so in anger or fear, but rather by reclaiming my power and discovering my own path while offering compassion for myself and the other party. I love collaborating and partnering with healthy people, and I now make sure it's not at my own expense. Is there anywhere in your life where you have been taught to suck it up? Do you know how it shows up in your life? Is there a pattern you fall into where you do things at your own expense? What's your relationship with boundaries?

I slowly realized that people were not letting me down, as it was my responsibility to be more mindful of the choices I was making. When I found that I did things at my own expense, I realized this was life teaching me to find my own path and take a healthier approach—one where I tapped into my own dreams and took bold steps, like writing these books and launching platforms to serve us from our hearts. I know, in my own heart, that people are starting to appear on my path, especially when I create boundaries. The wisdom of comedian John Cleese gives me hope to keep going: "When you collaborate with someone else on something creative, you get to places that you would never get to on your own. The way an idea builds as it careens back and forth is so unpredictable. Sometimes it depends on people misunderstanding each other, and that's why I don't think there's any such thing as a mistake in the creative process. You never know where it might lead."

EVERYTHING IS HERE TO BE DISCOVERED

When we put down the blueprint we were given of how our life should be, we release disappointment and open ourselves to possibilities. First-century Roman philosopher Seneca observed that "there are more things . . . likely to frighten us than there are to crush us; we suffer more often in imagination than in reality," and yet, the reality is that many of us do suffer and the pain incurred is real, no matter where the suffering is coming from. How we orient ourselves in relation to our suffering may be the single most significant predictor of our well-being and capacity for joy, but the greatest peril of misplaced worry is that in keeping us constantly focused on an imagined catastrophe, it prevents us from fully living and experiencing life.

When we start reinventing ourselves, we learn to integrate our failures as mere experiments that we can learn from and adapt. We no longer see our opportunities through the lens of mainstream assumptions, or measure how close or far we are from anyone else's achievements. We're focused on the outlier opportunities where we can create a healthy life based on our own unique boundaries. As a business, for example, we don't need to focus on looking around at what others are doing to see how we can outshine anyone else—rather, we can focus on bringing our passions to the people who care about what we produce for the community. Conscious leaders value dialogue and understand that deep relationships are foundational to building thriving lives and organizations, creating a world where we trust ourselves deeply.

There is no need to follow blindly when we learn to listen to our internal compass. In conscious relationships, people don't have to wait to be asked to share their ideas and give feedback. When we encourage people to make suggestions for improvements in the moment that they have an insight, we are much more likely to ignite creativity. We can't wait for someone else to take action or spend our life complaining about how broken the system is. It's up to us to navigate our own journey to a healthier world, where business creates genuine value for people and for society at large. We can be a part of something bigger than ourselves where work has a renewed meaning.

When you think about history, you can become a powerful creator in the stories of your life, your community, and whatever you choose to focus on. The key is to learn to think for yourself and do your own research. It's up to each of us to start questioning everything over and over, as well as trusting our intuition; that's because universal wisdom teaches us that there's a source to everything. There's a path beyond outrage and hate, whether it's of ourselves or others, that will open up when you do your work. Photographer and artist Carrie Mae Weems sums it up best: "Sometimes you sacrifice too much. You find yourself out on a limb and not knowing really quite how to get back down the tree. But it's the space that you're in because you have taken the risk. I'm not unaware of the sacrifices and, at times, whom your compassion hurts. It's not all moving in one direction. It's complicated, as the work is complicated." Don't be afraid to be judged for being who you are, as freedom begins with how courageous you're willing to be. Live fully, like your life depends on it.

The opportunity is to tap into our own heart—not with the

dreams and visions of other people, but by tapping into our own wisdom. Award-winning author Lynnda Pollio, in her life-changing book *Trusting the Currents,* shares, "It was the first time I realized how rich with possibilities life truly was, even if some were forced by unfortunate circumstances. Choice is a blessing . . . Knowing my heart though, that's what I was studying." Sometimes letting go is an act of greater power than hanging on and defending our choices.

In these books, you will discover how the old is becoming new again, and why self-trust is at the heart of everything. The question is, are you in tune and listening to what your heart is telling you and driving in directions that speak to your vision of the world you want to live in? Are you bursting at the seams to bring your vision to life and experimenting with all that is possible? It's easy to follow someone else, hoping for a break, but there is much beauty waiting for you to experience inside of you.

EXPEDITION 2

WHEN THE TIME COMES, LET IT GO

It's easy to look at a suitcase and see how much stuff we're bringing with us on a journey, but it's far more challenging to be aware of the layers of conditioning and programming that we're carrying deep inside of us, everywhere we go. There is no weight restriction when it comes to these programs that may be weighing us down. Becoming aware of why we're holding onto them and, at the same time, understanding what truly inspires us, is a journey in and of itself.

We can meet ourselves wherever and whenever we're ready to do our inner work and go explore what's deep inside of us. What nobody tells us is that this life is a fascinating experiment to simply be *experienced,* and each new day provides a fresh canvas on which to be present. What matters is that you're here to open yourself up to the opportunities on your own road of discovery. What path you take and what mindset you bring with you is up to you—and what you leave behind is also a choice, as you may not want to weigh yourself down with unnecessary baggage that's not actually yours to carry.

Take a moment and imagine you're about to embark on the journey of a lifetime. You've already packed your clothes, your shoes, your cosmetics, your books, and all physical items that you'll bring with you. How many suitcases are you bringing along? When you look at each of your suitcases, what size are they and how much do they weigh?

Now, it's time to pack your beliefs, your habits, your values, your mindset, your shadows, your attitude, your trauma, your grief, your hurt, your pain, your capacity to play, and your joy. Of those things, what percentage is healthy for your mind, body, and soul? And what percentage is unhealthy or toxic? Why did you choose each item? How much baggage are you bringing and why did you choose these specific items? Do your cases have any weight restrictions? If it's helpful to you, you can write this down and reflect on what you're carrying with you. Or maybe you have no baggage to bring with you, and there's nothing to write down and reflect on?

When we lighten our loads, we let what isn't serving us die a much-needed death. On this journey, we'll discover our love for life. Not the love tied in pink bows marketed on Valentine's Day or in romance novels, but a love that cannot be bought or packaged by an outside force or marketing genius. This love is at the heart of us and is in every villain and every victim who walks the earth. I've met people who declared they were all about love and yet their words fell short of their actual ability to love themselves and others. They told me I was a victim and they were correct, because in the story they created for themselves, they were the villain—which meant I was their victim. I could choose to stay in that story or walk away.

Our hearts see our dreams. The mind of another sees only *their* stories and their dreams. It's easy to be swayed by the dreams of others, but we're not here to play a starring role in someone else's stories. Of course, we can bend our ears and listen, but we can also allow their stories of villains and victims to pass through us like whispers of the wind. We have the freedom to choose how we respond and where our power rests.

Not all people who show up in our lives have pure intentions; some have never experienced real love and spread their hurt because that's all they know. A daughter of a narcissistic father may be shocked to find out that in her disdain of how her father treated her, she herself picked up the very same narcissistic qualities. How could she not, when that's all she was exposed to from a very young age? If she truly wanted to leave her baggage behind, she'd have to do the inner work to understand how she is showing up in the world and acknowledge that it doesn't need to be her way of life. The person who decides to tell us that we're a victim, on their own accord without being asked, is most likely feeling victimized in their own life.

This is where compassion steps in. This is an opportunity to realize that we don't need to "save" people—and that we can't, even if we try. Instead, we can find compassion for ourselves by questioning whether or not we want to carry baggage in our life that's not ours. True friendship has pure love running through its veins that carries healthy dialogue and connection to our hearts. When we feel resistance, there's something underlying that is asking to be addressed as an opportunity to grow—not always a wound or problem to be solved immediately.

It's up to us to hold our ground and not allow those with too much unhealthy ego to infect our dreams with their wounds. As we'll explore in the second book in this series, *F*ck the Bucket List for the Adventurer: Trekking into the Unknown*, those of us creating a healthy life are simply making space to cleanse and purge, not only our bodies but our thoughts and deep programming. We understand that we don't need to waste our energy throwing stones, judging others, or blaming anyone. We strive for unity within ourselves and each other, as we step away from a life of conformity.

OUR BAGGAGE DOESN'T NEED TO WEIGH US DOWN WHEN WE FIND OUR VOICE

A vital part of reimagining requires us to find the courage to challenge our beliefs and ask ourselves whether they are truly ours. We may have been told to aim for success, and we've probably been instructed on what success itself looks like, feels like, tastes like, and even what it smells like. We may have checked almost everything off the list: education, career, family, relationships, home, cars, clothes, vacations, promotions, friends, awards, bucket lists.

Yet we may find ourselves questioning what we truly want to achieve, and find we need to redefine what success really means to us. We may find ourselves increasingly yearning for deeper experiences alongside the awareness that continually numbing ourselves with superficial achievements and acquiring more and more possessions does not actually fulfill us. In our frenzy to achieve success on this materialistic and achievement-driven road, we may have lost vital pieces of ourselves, and may be ready to reimagine a healthy way forward.

The world we live in constantly tells us that more is better. There is only one winning team, one promotion, one award, and one best organization to work for. We are taught and conditioned to compete to be the best in the world, but what if we realize that we don't have to crush anyone else to be the only "winner"?

In many young people I had the opportunity to connect with

during my career at the networking company Cisco Systems, I witnessed an opportunity mindset. I worked with people who lived in some of the poorest slums in the world, and yet they inspired me with their hope and courage to pursue possibilities. One young man was an aspiring poet. When he knew he would be facing a great challenge the next day, he would slip one of his poems under his pillow at night, describing his anguish. After I shared with a group of youth in Kibera how to use social media tools to get their voices into the world, this young poet started posting his poetry online, where no one needed to know that he was living in a slum. He then started getting feedback and connecting with other poets, and also began getting invited to read his poetry in public, for which he would sometimes get paid. All he needed was his curiosity, imagination, connectivity, and a deep purpose to open new doors in his life. He may not have known where his next meal would come from, but he started to believe in his ability to share his voice.

As the voice of Hital Muraj, a global ambassador for youth, vibrates through the ethers, let's become aware that when we have a voice, we have a choice. "I would love to live in a world where we can each play our role and not have it be seen as Africans needing to be saved. What we need is opportunity. The way people can help is to be the voice. I want to be the voice of my people and our youth. What I know is that when you don't have a voice, you are in an unlucky situation because you didn't choose to be there, and yet, that is exactly where you are. We are all responsible for being the voices out in the world, to tell people that there is much more behind poverty than what is being shared in the media. We have amazing people with hope and skills who simply need the chance to make a life for themselves. And they want to solve their own problem, with coaching and guidance. They need job creation and skills development. And most importantly, they need to know that they matter. How do we ignite their fire and change their environment? By helping to give them a very loud voice in the world.

"We need more leaders in the world who are humble and who understand that we can learn from each other on this journey. It's no longer just about the title. People want to be around people they trust, not people they fear. Being able to emotionally connect with people, and being able to really define the challenges in this leadership position, are key. The new type of leader is great at listening and bringing people together with purpose."

PLEASE LEAVE YOUR LIMITING BELIEFS BEHIND

This is our opportunity to tap into a healthier way of living and working by shedding the theories, practices, programming, and mindsets that no longer serve us. We don't need to follow the latest fad. Rather, we can start listening more closely to our intuition and combine it with our rational knowledge to guide us to make healthier decisions. How can we embark on this path? By becoming aware of our limiting beliefs and understanding that they may not truly be ours. They don't need to be on our packing list for this journey, and they do not need to weigh us down.

1) Fear Is as Deep as the Mind Allows

My master's thesis was on the impact of television on the American political system, and it predicted much of what is happening today, thanks to the Greek philosopher Plato and the American author, educator, and media theorist Neil Postman. My continued doctoral research pointed to the influence the media would have on our society, but I fired myself from the PhD program because I was not allowed to do the research I had my heart set on. I had discovered that the media is owned by those who want to engender fear and this had huge implications on how we see the world through their lens of what they considered newsworthy.

After my oral exams, one of my professors took me into his office and told me that while he agreed with my research, he could not do so publicly in front of his peers. I had already passed my exams and all that was left was to complete my dissertation, but I could not be told what I could and could not bring to life in the one place that proclaimed freedom of thought but did not truly practice it. Plus, how could I teach others, which was my dream as well as writing, in an institution that tried to generate fear in me?

There are those who live off the energy of fear, and it is imperative for them that fear continues. When you live in fear, your brain shrinks. It literally shrinks. When that happens, your ability to see possibilities constricts. When you put your hands on the sides of your face, what do you see? You probably will only see what's in front of you and what is presented to you. You can't see up or down or right or left. When you live in a state of fear, your heart closes and your focus becomes surviving. Have you ever noticed that when you are stuck in fear, you can't see the possibilities in front of you? Everything seems bleak and hopeless. Anger and fear can keep you stuck and paralyzed.

Dr. Wendy Suzuki, NYU neuroscientist, professor, and author of *Healthy Brain, Happy Life*, found that when we adopt a mindset of gratitude and abundance, we eliminate the fear associated with words like "taxes" or "virus" or "death," or any other fear-inducing word. This mindset protects our brains and, in neuroscience-speak, we're decreasing activity in the area of our brains that processes fear—the amygdala.

The amygdala is not just a sensory area for fear, it also has the power to influence your physiology, triggering your heart to beat faster, causing you to perspire, and flooding your system with the stress hormone cortisol. When we counter this response with a mindset of gratitude, we don't have to live in a state of fight or flight. Dr. Suzuki's research has found that long-term stress literally kills the cells in our hippocampus, which not only contributes to the deterioration of our memory, but also zaps our creativity.

We don't have to join the violent fear movements and become warriors, or stand by helplessly and become victims, either. Let's allow our ability to imagine and reimagine lead us to take actions that bring us into alignment with how we want to truly live. We don't have to wait for someone else to show us the way, as they don't know what is in our hearts and minds. Only we do. And it's up to us to explore possibilities and be conscious of the role fear and anger have in our life.

We may feel that we cannot realistically pursue our dreams. I have spoken to so many people who started on a life path they wanted to follow, but then succumbed to the fear of failure or the pressure to take a job just to pay the bills. Unfortunately, this is often considered more honorable in our society than actualizing our dreams.

Society conditions us to fear. We are taught that danger is everywhere, especially when we're entering into the space of the unknown. We've been conditioned to embrace predictability and routine, while fearing that we won't get everything on our to-do list done. We too often come together to solve pending problems simply out of fear that the competition will outperform or out-innovate us. We tend to spend more time simply protecting and surviving than creating with pure joy and curiosity.

After one of my keynotes on the future of work and life, one participant shared the following insight: "I am so focused on this notion of fear as the biggest cause of failure and why people don't live to their full potential. People sitting in their cubes, hating their jobs, are afraid to make the leap, afraid to take a chance, to do what they love because they fear so many things . . . things that almost never come true." And it is true—most of what we fear or worry about never actually happens.

A few years ago I was invited to join a journey I never could have imagined taking. A group of seventeen women, known as the Jungle Mamas, were heading into the Amazon to learn about maternal health. I was busy working as an innovator-in-residence with a large company and didn't think I had the time to go. I had to sit with the idea for a while before replying. Eventually, I came to see it as an opportunity to address my fears, and I decided to take a leap and accept the invitation. That decision literally changed my life. When our small plane took off from Puyo, Ecuador, to head into the jungle, I turned my head and saw my old self waving goodbye, knowing that when I returned, I would be leaving a lot of my worries, doubts, and fears composting in the heart of the rain forest.

I faced some scary moments during my time in the rain forest, and I looked my fears straight in the eye. I discovered there is a whole other side to fear. Sure, there were scary snakes and bugs, but there was also immense beauty and tranquility. I realized I had dealt with bigger snakes in the business world throughout my career, and by taking a break from the daily noise of news and media, I understood that by facing my fears, I could tap into possibility, simplicity, and my ability to believe in and love myself.

Anyone who wants to make a difference has to address fear of the unknown. I learned that we didn't need to detox in nature but to remember that we're simply part of it—that there is intelligence there, which we can each learn from when we are ready. When we set out to change ourselves, by definition we are going to change into something that we can't yet describe—and that is inherently frightening for people, more so for some than for others. Some people stay in a job they hate for forty years, or a loveless marriage, because they're afraid of the unknown. We've created systems that prey on that fear as a function of propaganda about loyalty, but all this is changing for those of us who focus on health and well-being.

When we dig deep down and uncover the origins of our fears, we can start facing them head-on by naming them and acknowledging them. Can you, or have you already, started on the journey of addressing your fears? Are you allowing them to control your life? Our opportunity is to invest the energy necessary to create a healthy relationship with our fears and meet ourselves on the path of least resistance.

2) The (Often False) Sense of Safety

We've been conditioned to believe that we always need to be safe and careful, which on the surface makes sense. After all, we don't want to drive our car at high speeds on wet roads. But this conditioning gets taken much too far and we then become overly fearful, which keeps us caged.

Danger is everywhere, we're told. But what if that is nothing more than a limiting belief? What if being too safe is actually too risky? Being "safe" can be dangerous when our safety means locking ourselves in a cage, disconnected from our potential to soar. To open the cage door, we need to listen to our own internal compass.

Gaining approval from others doesn't always make us feel like we're living with purpose. More of us are spending our lives pushing back on boundaries, questioning the rules, and trying to find ways that work for us. This is part of the great shift that is taking place as we question the rules we have been handed.

We can choose to follow the status quo or we can break away. So much of it comes down to how we define success and failure. If our success is determined simply by comparing ourselves to everyone else, we'll always be a slave to the standards and needs of others. We'll always be supporting someone else's dream.

Some people have learned to lash out, judge, and fight for what is theirs, with the goal of taking another down so they can be seen and get their fair share of success. It's part of our collective story to be special, be right, win at all costs, and demand love. We've created comfort zones that are not always safe.

We are taught to stagnate, which leads to resistance of growth at the expense of safety. This is why there are experts now teaching us how to be human by being vulnerable and authentic. It has become a business for us to teach others to simply be human. Somehow, we have created a world where someone needs to tell us that it's safe to show up in every experience in our authenticity and vulnerability. What I've learned is that not only is it safe, but it is required to make the leap from where we stand today to a healthy, conscious society.

Trusting ourselves and creating trusted relationships are the gateway to living a healthy life. It's no longer necessary to remain stagnant in relationships that uphold false identities for the sake of safety. We are here to work through challenging people and experiences by not getting sucked into their drama or wanting to save them. And, ultimately understanding whether they are healthy or not for us. Most of us have been conditioned to believe that it's better to be in a relationship than to be single—and yet, how many people feel their partner dragging them down? Although revealing your truth in some situations may seem difficult—such as whether or not your relationship is healthy—it's worth the effort, as there is more joy, peace, and abundance to be uncovered. Your willingness to evolve in love with others is the precursor to more love evolving within humanity.

John Lennon's legacy reminds us that we have two foundational motivating forces: fear and love. "When we are afraid, we pull back from life. When we are in love, we open to all that life has to offer with passion, excitement, and acceptance. We need to learn to love ourselves first, in all our glory and our imperfections. If we cannot love ourselves, we cannot fully open to our ability to love others or our potential to create. Evolution and all hopes for a better world rest in the fearlessness and open-hearted vision of people who embrace life." And remember, too often being safe is very risky when we are caged within our limiting beliefs. How can we trek into unknown opportunities and possibilities when we're stuck in our comfort zone and a false sense of safety?

3) The Culture of Sameness

Isn't it fascinating how the most memorable line in Nora Ephron's script for *When Harry Met Sally* is not spoken by either Harry or Sally? Instead, it's an unnamed character who reacts to Sally's fake orgasm in Katz's Deli by saying, "I'll have what she's having."

We may have been conditioned to look outside of ourselves for guidance on what we need in our life. We may also always seem to want what others are having—even when what they appear to have is purely fake, just like Sally's orgasm. Report cards at school are a mechanism to measure and judge us according to everyone else. Parents monitor their children's progress by comparing their life achievements. This is a one-size-fits-all, cookie-cutter mentality, but in reality, cookie cutters only work when we are baking cookies. The irony is that we are not the same. We come in all colors, shapes, and sizes for a reason. There's no one yardstick for the growth of all people on the planet, and yet we go through life being expected to measure up to a "normal" bell curve. But who really wants to be normal these days?

Most likely, you've been conditioned to trust everyone else before yourself, raised into a culture of sameness and conformity where you're pelted with the latest fads and trends, and urged to keep up to belong. When you don't belong because of how you dress, where you live, or how you choose to live, you are shut out and become an outsider.

The truth no one tells us when we're kids is that we don't need to adopt someone else's best practices to have a fulfilling life. Our opportunity is to break the culture of sameness so that we can come into our own as creators, makers, and architects. It's our time to break the tyranny of being like everyone else by listening to the unique and beautiful voices that our souls whisper to us when we imagine. What is very much the same in all of us is our deep desire to experience love, to be understood, and to accept ourselves with no holds barred. What role, if any at all, does this belief play in your life?

4) Making a Living and Supporting Ourselves— Even at the Expense of Ourselves

On this materialistic road of success, there is an unspoken assumption that whoever dies with the most possessions and the fattest bank account wins. Everyone assumes the wealthy have it all, but what if having it all is a myth to keep us consuming and striving for more than we truly need? Dr. Bob Moorehead in the *Paradox of Our Age* shares, "We have bigger houses but smaller families; more conveniences, but less time. We have more degrees, but less sense; more knowledge, but less judgment; more experts, but more problems; more medicines, but less healthiness. We've been all the way to the moon and back, but have trouble crossing the street to meet the new neighbor. We've built more computers to hold more information to produce more copies than ever, but have less communication. We have become long on quantity, but short on quality. These times are times of fast foods; but slow digestion. Tall man but short character. Steep profits but shallow relationships. It is time when there is much in the window, but nothing in the room."

What allows us to tap into the deeper meaning in our life? We may be getting a monthly salary, but at what cost? We all talk about how we must have the material basics, like a roof over our heads and food to fuel us, and too often we mention Maslow's hierarchy of needs as our model of self-actualization. But what if there is a healthier model out in the world waiting for us to create it? Do we know what our "enough" is when it comes to how much money, clothes, work, education, friends, vacations, housing, and all that we need to live our life, and when enough is actually enough? And have we ever considered the wisdom of the indigenous practice of taking only what we need?

What we may need most is what we've been conditioned to fear—like curiosity, adventure, experimentation, vulnerability, play, authentic communication, time alone, and connection to life. We've been taught to mask our emotions; even our fear is to be private and discreet. We're told not to let anyone ever see our dirty laundry, and we're given endless tips for success and manifesting our reality. We've learned to find discomfort in authentic communication where we don't always openly share ourselves, even with ourselves.

We too often define ourselves through materialism, by how successful we are in the world, and split our existence into work and life. Our bank accounts help us fulfill our consumption as a way to help us feel connected through television, shopping, entertainment, and paying our never-ending bills, and being continually told to make sure we save for retirement. Meanwhile, our lives are craving intimacy, connection, joy, and deep meaning. But what if we are all here to contribute our gifts toward something greater than ourselves and we have the opportunity to do so?

You can turn these questions into an exercise when you go for a walk, or just take a pause. Whose story do you want to live? Is money an energetic tool for you, or is it a way of life? What drives your existence? Do you ascribe to limiting beliefs, or do your beliefs open up new possibilities? What is it that you need to live your life fully? I'll bet that when you truly invest the time in yourself to answer these questions and use your own metrics of success and failure, you will make healthier choices about how you spend your time and what's truly important in your life.

5) There Is a Seven-Step Formula for Everything—Including Being a Success

In our work life, it is often encouraged that we go to conferences to learn about best practices and case studies on how to achieve success. While there, everyone's on their best behavior, openly sharing the details of their wins without offering the full, true story of how they got there. Yet somehow, we elevate whatever is "tried and true" and believe that it can also work for us or maybe rub off on us, when that's rarely the case.

When people hear that I'm a published author, they often come to me for advice and ask me questions about my process and discipline. They also often leave disappointed when I tell them I have no rules to follow. If I wake up at two in the morning, then that's when the writing begins. If I could have my computer in the shower, that's probably where the downloads would flow the most. Sometimes I love long drives when I can drive fast and look out the window and process what is coming through me. I tell them that I have a love of writing and as such, it's not a chore that requires discipline. I came to this planet to provide medicine for the soul for those who are ready to put down the manual of success and become real and raw—but I don't know what drives anyone else to want to publish a book, so I ask a lot of questions and help them listen to themselves. My hope is that our conversations help them unlock their desires and begin to understand what they truly want to create in the world in their own way.

I help them see that instead of fighting the monster that tells them they are a fraud when it comes to writing, they can invite it in. That way, they can discover why the monster is haunting them, and even play with it to develop and grow on their journey. It is our choice to let go of the fear of being "found out" and, instead, stand out in our own light. Once we realize we're all in the storytelling business—the stories we tell ourselves as well as the stories we tell other people—we can befriend this monster and focus on the stories we want to tell and the experiences we want to create.

We may believe that fake news is real—but what about the fake stories and fake lives showcased in front of us as standards we should aspire to obtain? Why do some of us spend hours and days and even a lifetime berating ourselves for something we've done and feeling stupid and insignificant? It doesn't get more real than the state of mind we choose to live in, and who we choose to give our trust and power to. What if we make what's tried and true our way of life and learn through our experiences?

You'd be surprised at how many "successful" people have considered themselves frauds or fakes at one stage or another of their lives. Why does this happen? One key reason is that we have been conditioned to compare ourselves with others, to seek out very limiting metrics that are supposed to prove our worth—and that moment when we feel most vulnerable? That's when all our doubts flood our mind and often we become paralyzed by fear and insecurity.

When we can reacquaint ourselves with ourselves by understanding why we believe someone else holds our secrets, we can face our vulnerabilities. It takes effort to understand whether we are in or out of sync with who we are and why we're here at this moment in time. Many of us have been swimming upstream, placing societal norms ahead of our desires and gifts. Often, our responsibilities and lists cause stress between what we're supposed to be doing and what our hearts crave. Our souls may suggest to us that these obligations and successes were never ours to experience, and we silence them as much as we can, which ultimately brings us stress and dis-ease.

Societal stress around success has been passed down to most of us through the generations and can be seen, with healthy hearts, as a pattern that is simply waiting to be broken by our surrender to the unknown. When we're forced into an unnatural activity or belief, we become vulnerable and stop operating in our own best interests. This vulnerability is the entry point of discordance and dis-ease, and it takes us out of alignment.

When we follow the rules, our minds run on autopilot, unaware that we're allowing our powerful consciousness to continue in the ways of the past—our beliefs were set up through many previous experiences at different ages and different points in time. When we realize that we don't need to follow someone else's recipes, we'll tap into opportunities to use our mind to form our life, just as a sculptor shapes a sculpture from clay. Michelangelo, perhaps humanity's greatest sculptor, shared that "every block of stone has a statue inside it and it is the task of the sculptor to discover it . . . I saw the angel in the marble and carved until I set him free."

Author Rosamund Stone Zander in *The Art of Possibility* says, "Michelangelo is often quoted as having said that inside every block of stone or marble dwells a beautiful statue; one need only remove the excess material to reveal the work of art within. If we were to apply this visionary concept to education, it would be pointless to compare one child to another. Instead, all the energy would be focused on chipping away at the stone, getting rid of whatever is in the way of each child's developing skills, mastery, and self-expression."

Become aware of your thoughts and belief structures that this activity reveals to you when you're ready to face them as a sculptor of your life—then you will have the opportunity to understand your mindset. Perhaps you'll sense this is the moment you can become free of the prison of the past, composed of many old, outmoded, and limiting belief structures about you and the nature of reality in general.

6) Waiting to Be Picked

Rejection is a gift. Sure, our feelings may be a bit hurt when a person or organization doesn't accept us, but rejection creates space for something else that is more meaningful. It's not about winning that award or getting that job. It's about our own journey and making our way in the world in the best way possible, and moving away from seeking permission and safety, and trusting that someone else will take care of us.

We can harness the courage to experiment and learn how to *pick ourselves*. Choosing ourselves—which really means that we stop waiting for someone else to discover us, like the recruiter who has the perfect job for us or the client with the perfect project or the partner with the perfect life—can be one of the hardest things to do, for many reasons. This is especially difficult when the common story about rejection being a sign of failure is the story we continue to tell ourselves.

For me, waiting to be chosen was a limiting belief. Why did I need to wait for someone else to pick me for what I wanted to create with my life and my work? I had falsely assumed that someone else knew what I needed better than I knew myself. I started thinking more and more about why this was happening. Why were we even talking about who deserved that promotion at work? The twentieth-century model of life (what I call "command central") tries to keep us competing against each other and doubting ourselves. No one wants to be the last kid picked to join the team in a world where there is usually one award, one raise, one soul mate, or one promotion that you are conditioned to aspire to.

So much can shift when we change our mindset and move away from common definitions of success and failure. It took me over a decade to learn that for me, being safe is often risky, as it means that I have not explored my deepest dreams. Being courageous means stepping outside of our comfort zone and letting go of the fear of failure that we have been conditioned by. I keep firing myself from situations, relationships, and stories that are unhealthy and no longer serve me, that are not aligned with my deeper yearning for creation. I am learning what it means to be true to myself, and it's definitely not an easy road, but I have decided to choose myself by listening to my intuition and learning how to play like my seven-year-old self. And you can choose yourself, too.

Instead of ruminating on the worst thing that could happen in choosing yourself, allow yourself to wonder about what's truly possible. What's the *healthiest* thing that could happen for you? What opportunities are waiting for you to see them? When do you choose yourself?

7) Some Higher Power Knows What's Good for Our Bodies

Here is something interesting that you may not think is connected to you. From the time you were born, you were told what was good for you and what was bad for you nutritionally. One day, according to reports and research, coffee is good for you, and the next day, it's unhealthy. Look at the recent studies that have investigated sugar—not only how addictive it is, but that it is a major cause of cancer in people of all ages. We may think a food item has been prescreened and safe, but just a few years ago, the US Food and Drug Administration (FDA) admitted to feeding arsenic to chickens, which made me rethink who I trusted and why I was taught to put my trust in authority figures for my well-being.

Author Paul Levy wrote that "when we've been hoodwinked long enough, we tend to reject any evidence of the fact that we've been bamboozled—it can be too painful and traumatizing to realize that we have been fooled—which is to say that we then no longer prioritize finding out the truth." It can be challenging to know who to trust these days, so instead of trusting the people who gain from persuading us to consume *their* products, educate yourself and become an authority on what's healthy or toxic for *you*. Understand that there are governing bodies that are influenced by lobbyists and corporations to act in their best financial interests, which doesn't always honor ours. Become aware that marketing campaigns include people called "influencers" who get paid to say they love a certain product. Because we created this "influencer" and inadvertently gave them celebrity status, we have given away our power to some of the people we've come to trust most, putting ourselves in a very vulnerable position.

To be on a healthy path, I have learned to be cautious of who is truly trustworthy. I have researched and read information from those who say it's good or healthy and those who say it's bad or unhealthy. I gather information from all perspectives and do what I need to do to protect myself from what is toxic. I learned from publishers and ranchers like Bryan Welch, who shares his story in my book *Our*

Journey to Corporate Sanity that when you treat animals humanely, the soil on their farms is rich and healthy. We need bees to ensure our food supply is healthy because they're key to maintaining fertile soil and crucial to our food supply. There is magic beneath our feet that is here to teach us to pay attention to taking impeccable care of our planet, including our body and what fuels it.

What we put in our mouth can fuel us or destroy us from within. Pay attention to your nutrition. Make sure you know whether the soil your food was grown in used toxic chemicals. If you don't already, consider adding natural herbs to your meals, and become aware that everything can, and should, come from nature. Sure, some kids think that food comes from the supermarket, but isn't it our responsibility to teach ourselves and the people we love to know where our food is sourced?

The nutrition in our food has decreased dramatically in the past 100 years. Our society has come to love microwaves that zap our food quickly, but the real question is: Why can't we wait? Doesn't our body deserve healthy food? The food we put in our bodies, the thoughts we put in our minds, and the people we put in our hearts all influence our physical and mental health. Question everything and find sources that are not genetically modified or processed, for example, to decide what energy to ingest.

While talking openly about sex is taboo in many countries around the world, it's simply part of life. You may have been warned about sexually transmitted diseases (STDs) or told not to be promiscuous, but what no one teaches us is that sex is an exchange of energy with another person. When we agree to let a person into our body, there is not only the risk of diseases or viruses. Sex between two consenting adults is usually beautiful and does not need to be about fear. But just like asking whether we want to open our heart to another person, we can ask whether the person we're letting into our body is healthy or unhealthy for us. There is a deep connection with our physical, emotional, and mental health that we can consider when we think holistically.

Many countries have health care industries that wish to make money from people's illnesses. Health care is, after all, like any other business. They will do what they can to prescribe the latest drugs and medicines. They don't always care about our well-being as much as we do. I know because I was prescribed a medication that broke down my metabolism and forever changed my body. When I expressed concern to my doctor, he told me that I was a hysterical female and to trust him. I did my own research and realized that there was a side effect that was being hidden from the public.

Years later, there was a class-action suit against the drug maker, who admitted their wrongdoings. For me, it was too late. My body had forever changed from ingesting such a harmful medicine at the age of twenty-two. My doctor did what he could do to discredit the truth by making fun and berating a young woman, but I didn't let that stop me from searching for what was causing all these harmful side effects.

There is much we can do by harnessing and aligning our heart, intuition, mind, and body. What is interesting is that when we don't have access to health care, we search for alternatives independently— and what we often find is alternative healing that is available in nature. People who don't have health insurance or coverage search for alternatives and often find ones that work. When I went to the Amazon rain forest, I was amazed at how many natural resources they have access to for Western ailments like arthritis, depression, and so much more. I later learned about the healing power of mushrooms when I worked on the film *Fantastic Fungi: The Magic Beneath Us*. There is lion's mane mushroom for memory, turkey tail for immunity, and others that I could forage even in local forests. I was amazed that I could simply learn how to incorporate them into my daily nutrition.

I also learned a lot about hemp from working with a company that is building homes from natural materials made of hemp and lime. Isn't it interesting that hemp has been used by different cultures since 8000 BCE and that the US Declaration of Independence was written on hemp paper? Hemp requires less water than other industrial crops and none of the pesticides; it grows to maturity in just 90–120 days and also remediates the soil, making it an ideal rotational crop. One metric ton of hemp sequesters 1.5 metric tons of carbon.

As hemp grows in popularity around the world, I imagine there will be a transfer of production to natural resources. For example, the production of bottles might transfer from petroleum to hemp, which returns to the earth much faster. It will only take several months for hemp bottles to return to the earth and not pollute our oceans. And because hemp bottles deteriorate more quickly, they will provide us with fresher water. I predict we will see a concerted effort by the chemical and petroleum industries to discredit hemp-based bottles in an effort to justify the continuation of their own. Hemp will also begin to replace wood and products from other plants, such as cotton.

There will always be people who resist trusting an ancient ally like hemp, due to fear. Human nature, being what it is, prevents people from incorporating the truth within us. And yet, hemp is natural and can do much for human health as well as the environment.

Much changes when we listen to our body and realize that there is no one way for everyone. Become aware that what is good for one person is not necessarily good for you. Take advantage of what you feel guided to follow and whose interests you are supporting. Ask yourself, "Who am I allowing to have power over me?"

Your opportunity is to move into your body and heart, to discover your true compassion, and to understand that fear that surrounds you does not have to be yours. The key is to know who you are— not who others *say* you are. Being aware of how to balance your physical, mental, emotional, and spiritual body can create harmony and greater alignment in your life.

HOW WILLING ARE YOU TO LET GO?

The road to knowing what is truly in our own hearts, and on our authentic bucket lists, takes courage—the courage to face and relinquish the limiting beliefs that may have gotten in our way of living the life our souls desire. You may think a book should be written in a certain way, filled with quotes from all the right authors and stories from the highest authorities in life. You may have other beliefs that can get in the way of your enjoyment of this adventure. Whatever those beliefs are, write them down for yourself, question where they came from, and then find a way to lighten your load, if that's what you choose. Where we are going, you won't really need them. Understanding your attachments to beliefs, things, and people will help you in letting go of them, when you're ready. There are so many reasons why you can't do something, but ask yourself what the things are that you can no longer ignore, and why.

The definition of insanity is doing the same thing over and over and expecting a different result. So, you can keep taking the same baggage with you wherever you go, or you can raise your eyes to the horizon of possibilities awaiting you by stepping out of your recurring story. It's an opportunity to explore and reimagine what life means for you and how you want to spend your time on earth. Isn't it time for deep questioning and becoming aware of the walls that you have put yourself in, or the ones constructed on your behalf?

Yes, it takes courage, but one small step outside your day-to-day circle can lead to another. The key is to *begin*. When you are curious and tap into your imagination, you place your attention on a blank canvas of possibilities. You are the storyteller now, and you can imagine as many options as you like. You may ascend peaks or descend into valleys. You have free range. You can choose whatever interesting rocks or beautiful vegetation you like to fill your landscape. You can keep your garbage inside and let it rot—or discard it and compost your irrational fears, like I did in the Amazon rain forest.

The opportunity is always right here, right now, in front of you. When you can open your heart and mind, you'll be able to start observing the wonder inside of you. We all live in perpetual change and are always either ascending and descending on different tracks. We are in constant motion. We don't need to manage change; we need to learn to flow with it. Like the ocean, the waves will keep coming in; it is how we respond to each wave that matters. Do you trust the currents or do you fight them? Are you attached and hanging on to your baggage or can you lighten your load?

When we stand still and reflect, we're able to evaluate where we've been. This prepares us to be ready to integrate what is coming toward us, be it the next mountain to climb, storm to weather, or ocean to sail. We become more loyal to our true selves when we adopt an opportunity mindset, as we are born with the ability not only to imagine but also to reimagine what is possible. We can never be stuck when we are in flow and constant motion, ready to explore the horizon of possibilities.

The next time you face a problem, set your baggage on the ground, and before you jump to solving it, ask yourself, what is my opportunity here? Then decide what you want to bring along and leave behind, as you join your next expedition.

EXPEDITION 3

WHAT PROGRAMS ARE YOU TUNING IN TO?

For what we truly need in life, there is no universal manual or instruction guide that applies to each of us individually. We are programmed from an early age to achieve. We may find ourselves surrounded by goals and standards set by society and our cultural upbringing. We were probably taught to have clear goals, get good grades, be a good student, follow the rules so we could be a good citizen and have a good life. But who has deemed that this is the right formula for everyone? Who takes the time to know us, to communicate with our hearts, and to know what is the right path for us?

When we read a physical book, we can naturally see how many pages we've read and how many more unread pages to finish the book. When we read an e-book, at the bottom left-hand corner of the page there is AI (artificial intelligence) monitoring how slow or fast we read. Once it tracks our speed, an indicator notes how long it will take for us to finish the chapter. It can also estimate the percentage of the book we have read. But isn't the purpose of reading a book to fully experience it? By putting our focus on finishing, we are taking our attention away from the opportunity to fully participate and play with what we're experiencing from the book. Part of our conditioning teaches us that there's always a goal or a destination we must reach to succeed. But how does experiencing life fully fit into this story?

WE DON'T HAVE TO BE BOXED IN

Many of us have become disconnected from the natural cycles of the seasons. There are four seasons—winter, spring, summer, and fall—and within these cycles there are also moon cycles, sunrises, and sunsets. These are natural rhythms in the world we live in and are universal, no matter where we live. There are no calendars or clocks in nature—just light and darkness—and yet every living being manages to follow its own cycle and thrive in harmony without timetables or agendas.

We live in a world dominated by calendars and alarm clocks, with every moment of our time in need of being filled to be deemed productive, efficient, and important. By using alarm clocks to wake ourselves up and interrupt our sleep patterns, we are interfering with our body's natural rhythm to monitor and oversee our overall health and wellness.

We clock in and clock out as we try to conquer our never-ending to-do lists. A structured life is great to help organize groups of people, such as family and business, but when it takes over and drives us, it can become detrimental. This obsession with structure becomes a safety crutch that prevents our lives from having any kind of flexibility. In fact, it causes more anxiety and stress by adding pressure to make sure we adhere to it. Our devices are equipped with bells and notifications to keep us on schedule as we cut our days up into slices and segments. There is a certain amount of time to eat, a time to retreat on vacation, and then it's back to school or work. This is how the programming starts: at an early age in school.

Children have been over-scheduled with activities and after-school programs. Parents run ragged shuttling them from one event to another, from one practice session to another, leaving little flexibility in their routine lives, or time to ask questions and have conversations. And all of this can change in a flash as we've witnessed in our history. In this scenario, children then learn about the societal standards for productivity and don't get to experience or learn the benefits of rest and downtime—yet they deeply yearn to play and explore their imagination and curiosity. We all do.

When you think about it, we all live in a world full of boxes! Almost everyone has been conditioned to live in some type of box—a car, a tent, a yurt, a house, a mobile home, an apartment—and there is a mode of transportation to move us throughout our days as well, whether we drive, cycle, or take a train or bus. These are all "boxes."

We spend time in another box when we get to our destinations—the office, a hotel, a hospital, or school, for example. There, we may work in a cubicle or classroom and eat our meals at a table or in a cafeteria or at a restaurant. At the end of the day, we navigate our way home back in a box and interact with other boxes in our home such as a television, a computer, or another mobile device. During mealtime, we feed ourselves from a box and wash our dishes in another box and go to sleep in a box. Then when the time comes, someone else chooses another box or urn for us to rest in peace in, forever.

Each one of these boxes has invisible lines to protect the structure of society by controlling the status quo of conformity. Only *you* have the ability to see and recognize your own conditioning—where you've become trapped by rules that don't work for you. Only *you* can acknowledge, when you're ready and willing to ask questions and explore a way out of the box societal conditioning has locked you into, what society defines as good and bad, right and wrong, appropriate and inappropriate.

What's fascinating is that we all come into the world with our own stories, and some people find comfort in the current structures and conditioning. That's why I shared up front that these books are not for everyone and dedicated them to the millions of people who are ready to open ourselves to trek into the unknown and un-condition from what no longer serves us. The future is mostly unknown because while we can say or sing words like love, peace, and harmony, we have yet to truly live them on a planet where many of us find ourselves surviving, divided, or fighting for our life. The fact that everyone is at our own intersection is something I've had to come to terms with long ago, which is why I prefer dialogue and exploration over divisive arguments where one person is *right* and everyone ends up losing. At the same time, we are each being called to do what we believe is healthy for us and to respect that implicitly.

We have an opportunity to make our own observations and choices. These are times that call for us to dig deep and find the stillness and the strength to follow our intuition and heart. It is up to each of us to turn the alarms and the notifications on or off, as only we know when we're ready to pause, breathe, find our center, and ground ourselves. And when we do, we can become aware of our unique gifts and talents, as well as our ability to be present with them.

I've been shown that the more we fight the system, the more fighting we will have to do in every box that constrains us. And that there's another way where we don't need to fight anymore when we learn to tap into our natural resiliency. What kind of life do you want to usher in?

Feeling into Frustrations Is Actually Healthy for Our Souls

There is a way out of the box—but it is up to you to become aware of when it gets too uncomfortable, too stifling, and when your spirit is frustrated with how your life is unfolding. It takes courage to admit to yourself, "This is not working for me. There has to be something healthier that will make me whole, and I am willing to open myself up to exploring and discovering it."

I know because I used to work all the time as I drank the company's Kool-Aid. A typical workweek often required working ten-, twelve-, and fourteen-hour days, and flying over the weekend to get to whatever meeting I was scheduled to be at next. Showing up in offices around the world with unhappy people, where the reward for doing a good job was to drink too much, eat rich food, and do more work. The programming of performing and excelling ran deep in the psyche, and I could not see how delusional this narrative was as I was in the midst of believing that in order for all of us to succeed individually, our company needed to continue to grow and win. And I found the same to be true regardless if it was a large corporation or a non-profit I was working with.

The only professional coach I ever had was a destructive force in my career; she had never worked inside a corporation and gave me some really bad advice about dealing with my boss, which totally backfired and cost me my promotion. She was hired to be an expert to give advice, but her execution taught me a lot about how important it is to ask questions. Everyone who touches our lives teaches us something important that we are meant to learn. Learning the lesson and self-forgiveness is one of the healthiest ways to honor ourselves. In a world full of experts telling us what's the healthiest course of action, particularly if you're not sure about something, it is key to trust your intuition. When there's a feeling you have deep in your bones, trust the part of you that is all-knowing, and that instinct can guide you in uncertain times.

It's funny that when we reflect on how we got here, we are often shocked to wake up to what is truly going on. It's like rubbing our eyes after a bad dream and wondering, "What just happened?" And there are not many people to talk to as most people don't want to acknowledge what is really going on.

Very few people are willing to walk out of what is considered success. But even in the darkest hours, we can access the seeds of hope and courage that are in us. I learned to trust the currents of life, even when I wasn't sure where they were taking me—because I'd started to see what worked for me and what didn't, despite what the experts and authority figures prescribed. I now know that I couldn't openly write and help myself and others unless I experienced this world myself. By doing my own deep work and asking tough questions, I discovered that I came to this planet not to be an executive in a large corporation, but someone who provides medicine for the soul through writing articles and books and providing guidance to other souls on this path.

There Is a Balance in Everything

Being positive and staying in balance is a powerful energy source—but being programmed to fixate on the positive and disregard the whole gamut of what it means to be human is a constant reminder of what we are missing and what we lack. It is not very useful, as each one of us is a little bit imperfect and has lessons to learn throughout our lifetime. It's kind of funny when we really stop and think about all the programming that we've been exposed to, and how hardwired it has made us to not question the source of these beliefs.

Everything in life is made up of positive energy and negative energy. You may be familiar with the saying, "birds of a feather flock together." What it means is when we feel down or pessimistic—which are negative energies—we'll often attract similar people into our lives, as well as unwanted events and incidents that vibrate to the same energetic frequency. However, the good news is that we have a choice. We can choose to have an opportunity mindset as our vibration and attract positive energy into our lives.

It's about becoming aware of our mindset and what boxes we have confined ourselves within. Some of the most constricting barriers we build are not made from material items like steel but are rather infections of the mind, such as believing stories that jail us in an invisible prison of belief. There is always a way out and toward self-awareness and creation. Asking yourself questions starts to shift your current state of mind. Ask yourself, how am I feeling about my life right now? Can I take a pause in my life right now, and become aware of the boxes, if any, that are restricting me? Why am I feeling boxed in? And can I imagine a healthier state of mind for me? What would it feel like?

We are powerful beings and no box is strong enough to keep us in a tightly structured system that controls and limits us. You already hold the key to discovering your path and authoring your story. Up until now, this little-known fact has been kept secret from the majority of the population. No one teaches us that we hold "The Key." Yet, to find the key that will unlock our minds, we must be ready to answer the question, "Am I ready to take impeccable care of myself and be fully responsible for my well-being?"

THE TRUTH IS THAT NO ONE KNOWS WHAT IS RIGHT OR WRONG FOR US

Did you know that when most of us make decisions and take action, 95 percent of our decisions are made with limited conscious awareness? What this means is that the beliefs that have been programmed into our minds have created automated responses for how we react to situations and the people we bring into our lives.

William Shakespeare wrote, "There is nothing either good or bad but thinking makes it so." While right and wrong, or good and bad, on a universal level makes sense, when we dig deeper we can understand Shakespeare's insight that this also creates automatic, canned responses that have been programmed into our minds. The beliefs that have been instilled in us matter, and it takes hard work to question whether they are actually ours. Only *you* know what and who is for you and what and who isn't, no matter how much anyone tries to convince you otherwise.

As mentioned earlier, advertisers tell us what foods are good or bad for us, but do they know our body as well as we do? All you can do is to always be aware of the source your food—make sure it comes from healthy soil—and become aware of how your body reacts to what you're consuming. Does the food you're consuming make you sluggish or does it energize and fuel you? Are you ingesting healthy or toxic ingredients?

Our societal conditioning has taught us to *blame*. Go online at any moment and you'll see posts of shaming. Most recently, I saw one that brought this home. Someone invited me to watch the CEO of Coca-Cola "lie and squirm his way out of some tough questions" that everyone should be asking his company. They wanted Coca-Cola to face the same kind of health scrutiny that big tobacco has been subjected to and start having health warnings listed on their pretty red cans. But why can't we move beyond shaming, blaming, and judging? When we continue to consume toxic beverages with high sugar content, which are indisputably unhealthy for our bodies, there will always be some company that will continue to sell and market it. What's the point of shaming or blaming a company for *our* unhealthy choices? It is time to become aware of the fact that when the foundation of our house is rotten, we don't build another story.

Instead of getting sucked into fighting the system, reimaging it or taking others down, we can learn to focus on what's within our control. By not consuming any product that is harmful for our health, we don't even need a warning label. Our power rests in becoming aware of what is in every product we consume. Our purchasing power lies in not buying what harms us or our environment, and not buying what we don't need. What if we knew ourselves enough to not only take what we need but also to make conscious choices about every aspect of our life?

As mentioned earlier, information is all around us, and the more we educate ourselves, the healthier we will be. For example, properties extracted from certain herbs, such as holy basil, can boost our immune system. Ginseng also lifts our immunity. Turkey tail mushrooms have been effective with breast cancer. Certain nuts and berries are very healthy and boost our immune systems right away. There is innovation taking place with mushrooms that can serve as alternatives to toxic pesticides and help with cleaning up oil spills. We control the volume of the noise in our world, and when we don't believe we do, it's time to question who holds our power and why we have given away our control. Everything is here to be discovered, and what's old is becoming new again!

BECOMING AWARE OF AUTOMATIC RESPONSES AND BLIND SPOTS

Often it's being unable or unwilling to see or experience life fully that causes us to stumble along our path. So, our opportunity is to become aware of our automatic responses and blind spots. Have you ever been in a situation where you felt like you were going through the motions on autopilot? Have you ever been in your car driving and when you got to your destination, you felt numb and didn't remember the journey? It happens to all of us as we rush through our lives pursuing what we were told was good and honorable for us. But when we step out of the structures and belief systems that we were conditioned to believe in, we can start asking questions like "Is this for me or is this not for me?"

The most foundational relationship we can have in life is with ourselves, and enriching that relationship requires relearning what inspires us. Knowing what and who is healthy for us, and what and who depletes us. It's important to learn where our automatic responses and limiting beliefs originate. We can not only question our belief systems—particularly if they're limiting us—but also examine how and why we respond to them the way we do.

So much is possible when we choose to put down the manual of success. Can you imagine a world where children are taught to distinguish between what is healthy and what is unhealthy for them, whether it's people who become trusted friends, beliefs they adopt, or food they consume? It's one thing to teach a child that fast food or alcohol may be bad for them and vegetables are good for them, but a whole world of opportunity awaits in helping children become aware of what is healthy or toxic for their hearts (people), minds (thoughts and beliefs), bodies (products and food) and souls (imagination and adventure). But first, before we start teaching anyone else, let's learn it for ourselves. How can we teach anything we don't practice ourselves?

Pursuing what is meaningful to us can recharge our batteries and lift our spirits, so we can be resolute in our determination to follow our intuition. The key is to begin taking action, because there's a window of opportunity open to us now, offering to move us away from simply reacting to life and into experiencing it fully. As there is no one universal formula for all of us, please customize these questions as you see fit. You can start taking action by exploring the following:

→ Self-care is an ongoing practice to truly know yourself and what keeps your body and mind healthy. What practices, if any, help you take impeccable care of yourself? Are you living the life you want to live, or are you conceding to the system? When was the last time you experienced yourself as fascinating? Tell a story about the role of self-care in your life.

→ Relationships are key to your well-being. Do you trust yourself? Now, what about the people in your life: are they healthy or toxic for you? Are there any patterns surrounding your relationships? How can you cultivate and foster healthy relationships? What's your vision for balance within yourself and with others? Tell a story about the relationship you want to have with yourself and the people in your life.

→ Lifestyle focuses on how you spend your time. What does fun and play look like for you? What role does work play in your life? What role does community play in your life? Tell a story describing your lifestyle and what's in balance and what's out of balance.

→ Purpose focuses on why you are here and goes beyond a role, a title, or an obligation. What's your mission? No matter how big or small, do you know why you are here? Did you come here to suffer, serve, create, or all of the above? If you could be living the most meaningful life, what would it look like? How far or close are you from what you imagine? Tell a story about living a purposeful life.

You may have been taught that success is good and failure is bad—but what happens when you become aware that there are only life lessons on the road to creating a healthy and balanced life? To know what is healthy for us, we learn how not to sabotage ourselves along the way. It's a gift called life and it's up to each of us to decide how we want to live and who we want at our side. This is not a lighthearted exercise, but it does offer you the opportunity to clear out anything that has outlived its purpose.

Becoming Aware of Whether Our Past Is Haunting Us

What if most people are simply doing the best they can? What if instead of judging or blaming, we realize—even when we get hurt or disappointed—that we have to understand our role in every situation and relationship? Can you even imagine what could happen if we started to question the beliefs and programs running in our mind, and realize they were planted there through our societal conditioning or ancestral past?

That's what happened to me. I started to observe my thoughts and beliefs, and began questioning whether they were actually mine. I looked at some of my deepest fears and could map many back to family members and stories that I'd heard or read. I started distinguishing between beliefs that were my own and beliefs that were planted deep inside of me. Sometimes this practice became overwhelming—but it was important to let go and release the beliefs and voices that were harming me and understand the root of where they came from.

I'd often hear this voice telling me I needed to try harder and to not trust people at face value; it took years to figure out that it was my grandmother's voice buried deep inside of me with a long ancestral lineage of suffering and survival. While my grandparents escaped Vienna in the Second World War, their parents believed Austria to be a cultured country. Having lost a son in the First World War, my great grandparents believed they were safe staying in their home country and were untouchable.

When I was studying at the Hebrew University of Jerusalem in my twenties, my Aunt Dita came to visit from New York. She asked me to take her to Yad Vashem, the World Holocaust Remembrance Center, where we found records documenting her parents' deaths in a Nazi concentration camp. My cousin, Stephen Fry, later documented our family history (on my father's side) in a BBC show called *Who Do You Think You Are?* While doing research for the show, he not only found the address of our great grandparents' house, but a young woman living there who had put up a poignant plaque on the house commemorating all who had lived there and had been killed in the Holocaust, including our great grandparents themselves—Berta and Samuel Braun.

I vividly remember walking up the stairs to her apartment and hearing the voices of all those who were taken to their deaths whispering in the hallways. I later became aware that these were voices I would often hear whispering to me in my day-to-day life and were ingrained in my psyche. What we aren't taught is that many of us carry ancestral trauma within us and those unidentified voices run through our psyches, especially when they're associated with deep fear or pain.

I was an avid reader from a young age, and at the age of fourteen

I started reading books about the Holocaust. For some reason, I also started reading many books not only about cults, but about families that hired people to deprogram and free their loved ones from cults. I then went on to read biographies and autobiographies about atrocities in Cambodia, Argentina, the cultural revolution in China, Sudan, South Africa, Rwanda, Congo, indigenous peoples in so many places, and so many others in the world where people warred over deep ideological divides. I couldn't understand why we, as human beings, often chose darkness regardless of country, nationality, or race. Our deep divides were evident when we followed others blindly, and I continually had this deep knowing, as I read more and more of the same human behavior, that it didn't need to be this way. It was evident that we can choose a path of peace and harmony, first within ourselves before changing anyone else or the world.

What I had learned from my extensive research was that ancestral imprints are a very important aspect of how we experience our lives. They are formed through ideologies, perceptions, emotions, reactions, and deep programming that become a real part of our identities. When a very significant emotional response arises through our experiences, an imprint is formed in our psyche that impacts our past, present, and future. These imprints are like building blocks inside of us, strengthening their voices within our minds, and as they do, they carry more weight in how we respond to the external world. Some of the identities that we assume throughout time run subconsciously in the background of our minds. When we become aware of them and how they shape our lives, it becomes possible to shift the experiences we create through them.

We may find ourselves blaming our pasts, our partners, or our parents for suppressing our happiness. But we all have the choice to move from feeling victimized to questioning ourselves. Why do we feel this sense of blame, and where does it originate from? What fears or past programming are holding us back? How is our perceived sense of responsibility and societal expectations getting in the way of our showing up fully and connecting with others in the present moment?

For me, it was time to break free. It was such a joy to meet this young Austrian woman who knew the history of the people who had lived in Rembrandtstrasse 33 in Vienna and wanted to remember our humanity through acts of kindness. We talked for a few hours and brought healthy energy to my great grandparents' house—as our generational connection was about moving forward and healing—by finding common ground and realizing there were no sides dividing us. We focused on what we were creating in the world, while respecting the past but not staying in it.

When I left her apartment, I walked down the stairs and had a cry of release as I walked out the front door, looked at the plaque outside, and knew in my heart that I had a big job to do in the world when I was ready. I had to do my own work first—starting with facing my shadows. At that moment, an old man walked by, and our eyes locked in a deep remembrance. I decided I didn't need to carry this pain and hurt within me, but I didn't fully know what that meant. I guess the first step was becoming aware of the programming in my own mind and how it impacted my life.

Being face-to-face with my ancestral past made me more aware that I didn't need to bring the trauma everywhere I went—and as someone whose first memory in life was of war, being safe had a very different meaning, one of survival. Had "my side" lost the war when I was three years old, I wouldn't be here and you wouldn't be experiencing this book.

I learned that this is why I am here now—to simply serve as a guide to help anyone who is ready to discover inner peace without needing to war or fight for our life. I realized that I didn't want to be part of a club that knows better than everyone else and to live by rules and beliefs that are harmful to my soul. I was willing to look at my own ignorance and powerlessness so I could not only address my own limitations but also see the opportunities. And I increasingly became aware that it's not my job to change anyone's mind or challenge or instruct anyone in how to live. When we become aware of the baggage we're carrying around and where it originates from, we are free to decide whether we want to bring it with us or not. May you be willing to observe, listen, and understand what voices are whispering to you. And be willing to be turned inside out and upside down and find the places you can crack open to let peace and harmony in. This is true alchemy.

Life always gives us an opportunity to feel into every identity we have created or have been boxed into—be it wife, husband, son, daughter, sister, friend, neighbor, employee, leader, teacher, student, survivor, victim, victor, narcissist, philanthropist—and observe which one speaks the loudest to us. It takes curiosity and courage to understand which of our identities are still entangled within us and tied to our trauma or wound, and which are boxes or roles that we don't want to carry in the same way. For example, we can set boundaries in any situation or place that may be out of balance. It's much harder to walk away from family or a long-term partner, but if the way we're reacting creates the same results and pain, the question is, what will it take to break the cycle? We can walk away or we can take different approaches, like getting help, to change our patterns by improving our communication skills, for example.

Seeing our patterns, and where we may be stuck, means that we can see the imprints or stories that are subconsciously siphoning our energy and keeping us chained to our baggage. Although it may seem challenging to face our shadows, this is an opportunity to release the chains and trek into the unknown, while addressing our past trauma, weakness, or shame in healthy ways. Can you even imagine transitioning into a harmonious and peaceful reality by becoming self-aware? It is possible. Anything is when we put our whole self into it.

QUESTIONING EVERYTHING IS A HEALTHY MUSCLE TO FLEX

On my path, I met many people who tried to convince me that they had my answers, but they didn't take the time to become aware of my questions. I had to do my work to uncover what and who was healthy and toxic for me. There were some extremely challenging times when I questioned why I gave my trust to such untrustworthy people. They were not bad people, as they were doing their best—they were simply not for me.

It would have been much easier for me to sit back quietly and observe the world privately, but I decided to walk my talk by documenting my discoveries through writing books and doing my work. I'm not better than anyone, yet I'm very different from a lot of people around me. I've been told many times that I'm way ahead of my time, and to be honest, all I understand from that is that people feel safe with what we know. It's easier to live in a world of good and bad than to shift to becoming aware of what's healthy or unhealthy for each of us. Every business journal will highlight the importance of innovation, and yet the reality is that most people resist change because we have been led to feel comforted by the way things already are and fear not knowing how to change ourselves. It's easy to think we're safe with any limiting belief we adopt.

When I became aware that the increase in breast cancer is correlated with toxic chemicals in mainstream deodorants, I started questioning my automatic response to what I was told was good for me and who I should trust. Magatte Wade, founder and CEO of Skin is Skin, made me aware that I shouldn't apply any substances to my skin that I can't eat. I started to question and become aware rather than accept the status quo, especially when I saw it hurting so many people around me. I knew there were healthier options for dealing with body odor, which I was taught was bad and embarrassing. I then realized that the price of perfection—not having body odor (bad) and concealing my sweat (good)—was the standard I didn't want to live by if it cost me my health. There are now effective natural deodorants on the market, which are healthy for the human body, including coconut oil that comes from nature.

Would you consider swallowing a spoonful of toxic chemicals? I would hope your answer is no—but in many ways, smearing them under your arms in the form of an antiperspirant may be just as bad for you. Research by Philip Harvey, PhD, editor in chief of the *Journal of Applied Toxicology*, found that some compounds used in antiperspirants are absorbed and stored in fat cells, which are prevalent in the underarm area. Did you know that antiperspirants could cause or contribute to developmental or reproductive issues, as well as cancer?

A California jury awarded $29 million to a woman who said that asbestos in Johnson & Johnson's talcum-powder-based products caused her to get cancer. And who told us that spraying Roundup to destroy weeds in our yards was actually "safe"? Since Roundup first entered the market in the 1970s, Monsanto has denied claims that it causes cancer, insisting in an advertisement that Roundup is "safer than table salt." But according to internal Monsanto emails, now known as *The Monsanto Papers*, it has known for several decades that Roundup (glyphosate) causes cancer. Rather than informing consumers about the glyphosate cancer risk, Monsanto buried the information as sales of Roundup skyrocketed.

There's a Cost to Everything

If those who believe in a healthier path sit back or hide, nothing will shift, and the status quo will prevail—but when we share healthy news and healthy ways of living, especially through healthy networks, conversations, and books, much becomes possible. We can then start finding and connecting with each other, walking together in a healthier direction. It takes small steps to believe that we can create a healthy life and relearn what works for us and what doesn't.

I'm sure autopilot is healthy when you're a pilot, but when we're navigating our lives, what is healthy for us? What is unhealthy? These are the questions guiding me to greater awareness—what are yours? How do you truly want to show up in our world, and with whom?

As you embark on your path, it's up to you to decide whether or not you will let go of what no longer serves you. It's your choice: continue playing a part in someone else's manual about how your life is supposed to be lived, or look inward and discover a healthier direction. To make space to reimagine and create, your opportunity is to first deal with your own limiting beliefs and focus on unlearning and un-conditioning those things that are now—or perhaps have always been—harmful to you.

I am sharing with you the top things I realized I had to un-learn in order to live my best life. I encourage you to personalize these suggestions and questions, as only you know what speaks to your soul. Anything learned can also be unlearned.

Un-conditioning #1 — Being busy doesn't have to be a way of life. Author Tim Kreider shares that busyness is usually self-imposed: "Busyness serves as a kind of existential reassurance, a hedge against emptiness; obviously your life cannot possibly be silly or trivial or meaningless if you are so busy, completely booked, in demand every hour of the day." Being busy, in some circles, has become the badge of honor to show how important we are.

Many of us are even too busy to think about or practice self-care. We may be running from meditation class back to the office and then to the gym, before heading home to work some more. But being over-scheduled simply leads to burnout. And this is nothing new. Author and television producer Shonda Rhimes is often quoted for pointing out that "You can waste your lives drawing lines. Or you can live your life crossing them."

Here are some questions to ask yourself: Who do you spend time with? Where do you work and who do you work with? What do you consume? How much do you play? Are these things aligned with what you want to create during your lifetime? It's really hard to change your story if you are always going to *consume* as opposed to *create*, which can be terrifying as there is no manual for what you can create.

Un-conditioning #2 — Please remind yourself that you don't necessarily have to follow instruction manuals unless you are assembling furniture or navigating a ship. It can be very helpful to receive suggestions and guidelines, such as I am offering in this book, but there is no manual universally applicable to everybody, and that is what so many so-called experts keep trying to sell us. Ask yourself who benefits from their expertise, and do they care about you as much as you do?

Consumption is the emotional equivalent to our relationship with comfort and security—a desire for a nicer restaurant, a second house, flying in first class. Our social status matters. Fame, power, and ego are rooted in the accelerated pursuit of material things, which ultimately helps determine our ranking in the social world. We have learned to consume for the sake of comfort, building our security at the expense of others and the earth that sustains us. Who you know, where you work, what you do, where you shop, what you buy, where you live, and what you consume all matter deeply if you are climbing the ladder to success.

Branding is very much a buzzword at the moment in the marketing world and has now filtered into everyday conversation. Did you know that the word *brand* is from the ancient North Scandinavian term meaning "to burn"? It actually refers to the practice of using branding irons on livestock to burn the farm's name onto hides. It is also used in the practice of craftsmen engraving their names into products and personal belongings.

Modern branding has evolved out of something to desire, as celebrities endorse products associated with themselves. The goal is to seduce consumers to want the same material possessions as their idols, under the delusion that they bring happiness and fulfillment. It's a great human misconception to seek something outside ourselves to worship. Being inspired or enjoying something that has meaning to you is important, but it's also important to resist elevating it to an unhealthy obsession.

We can easily define ourselves through our overconsumption of brand symbols—from fashion, to dining, to technology. Owning the latest Gucci purse, the newest iPhone, or eating at the Ritz-Carlton Hotel in an effort to personify the trendiest brand labels because we believe it will bring respect and prestige is a fallacy. Paying for overpriced goods is just paying huge sums of money for items.

This is not a judgment but a reality that's prevalent and ever-increasing without a ceiling to stop it. It has become rampant, with no end in sight. In China, for example, people are selling a kidney to buy an iPhone, and girls are working in clubs to own a $40,000 Louis

Vuitton handbag to hang from their shoulder. The world's greatest consumers are in China, where people have spent over $102 billion on overseas travel alone. Gucci, Mercedes, Rolex, and Louis Vuitton are highly desired because these brands can make the poor appear rich, and obtaining a lavish lifestyle is held in high regard.

When we become increasingly aware that our entire culture is built on work (making money to pay the bills), distraction (modes of entertainment), and the quest for happiness, we may find ourselves not wanting to participate in an economy that thrives only because people buy products, services, and medication that help us avoid pain. Ask yourself, "Do I know what I value and how I want to live my life? Am I following someone else's manual of success or am I creating my own?"

Un-conditioning #3 — We don't have to suffer through life and remain hidden. You may have been conditioned to wear mental armor and project various masks to hide what you're feeling—to hide who you *really* are. You may have been told that emotions have no place in cultural and business interactions, but at the same time, you certainly cannot deny your emotions, as they will work through you and affect your decisions whether or not you are even aware that they are doing so.

If you were brought up in Western society, you have probably been taught from birth to avoid pain at all costs and that there's a pill for anything that ails you. It has been so deeply rooted in your conditioning that you may not be aware of how often you avoid pain. Becoming aware of what you were socialized and conditioned to practice, wherever you are in the world, is key to understanding how to unlearn it. Is it truly better to suck it up and avoid pain, or is it possible to simply experience life and have a healthy relationship with your deep-rooted fears or sadness?

The second I started doing my inner work and questioning everything, my entire life imploded. I was holding on so tightly to everything, from my relationships to my lifestyle, that it was uncomfortable. Everything changed in a flash. And even when I thought nothing else could possibly change, everything crumbled away. I realized that I never fit into the existing model of how life should be. But there were a lot of perceived comfort and safety nets embedded deeply in the old model. When I moved out of my comfort zone, there were risks I took, and there were always consequences as well. What I learned was that each one of us can walk our own path, if and when we choose to. It's very personal.

Author Pema Chödrön suggests that "feelings like disappointment, embarrassment, irritation, resentment, anger, jealousy, and fear, instead of being bad news, are actually very clear moments that teach us where it is that we're holding back. They teach us to perk up and lean in when we feel we'd rather collapse and back away. They're like messengers that show us, with terrifying clarity, exactly where we're stuck. This very moment is the perfect teacher, and, lucky for us, it's with us wherever we are." Ask yourself, "What role does suffering play in my life? Am I in touch with my gut feelings? Do I need to relearn how to tap into my heart as well as become aware of any programming of my mind?"

Un-conditioning #4 — Comfort zones can be uncomfortable. Our opportunity is to open ourselves to exploration. It's about becoming aware of our unconscious habits, like driving somewhere and realizing later on we weren't even aware of how we got there. It is about opening ourselves to life.

It's up to us to open our hearts and accept that the pain and challenge in our lives actually reflects the depth of our caring and commitment to life. It's part of the cycle that charges imagination and creativity. Much can happen when we unleash our passion for creation—without it, we may find ourselves scared, lost, lonely, or hurt. There are people who want to set people against each other—for them to be scared enough to consume more fear that then drives up the stock price of their material goods, for example. Fast food companies exist because there are people who consume fast food for their own reasons. They will continue to exist when we continue to support them; and the same applies to feeding fear.

This journey is very personal and is prone to taking many twists and turns as we open ourselves up to new opportunities and possibilities. It's about asking questions, creating meaningful opportunities, and connecting first with ourselves and then with others on the journey of creation. For some reason, many of us have a strange and subliminal relationship with what and who we consume. Do you know why you feel drawn to purchase something or to bring a person or a belief into your life? There is a subtle difference when we're conscious and aware of the choices we make, from what we decide to buy to the people we engage with and the communities we're attracted to.

Un-conditioning #5 — No one knows us as well as we know ourselves. It's time to trust ourselves and let our inner voices and intuitions guide us. We can allow ourselves to dedicate time and energy to drop the mechanical habits we have learned so that we can tap into our creativity and our own genius. Ask yourself, "What is blocking me from letting my creativity and genius flow, and what can I do to unleash it?"

While we've been conditioned to fight for our lives, or fight the *good* fight, most battles with others are not worth fighting. What does it really mean to spend our lives being right when we can learn not to engage in toxic arguments that create more division? Can you stay focused on what is important to you during challenging times and align yourself with your own soul mission of why you're here? Stay strong in your connection to your intuition and learn to question and go to the root cause of issues, as being right is temporary and healthy dialogue is your opportunity to break free from all the conditioning.

In an article in *Life* magazine called "Old Man's Advice to Youth: Never Lose a Holy Curiosity," Albert Einstein wrote, "The important thing is not to stop questioning. Curiosity has its own reason for existence. One cannot help but be in awe when he contemplates the mysteries of eternity, of life, of the marvelous structure of reality. It is enough if one tries merely to comprehend a little of this mystery each day. The ideals which have lighted my way, and time after time have given me new courage to face life cheerfully, have been Kindness, Beauty, and Truth."

Un-conditioning #6 — Not everything is as advertised, and some products and people can be toxic to our health. Living in awareness and being conscious of what you are consuming is key. Are you aware of your limiting beliefs and the role they are playing in your life? Are you charging them rent for the space they take in your mind? You don't have to allow them to weigh you down. What and who are you choosing to bring with you, and is there anyone holding you back? Endings can be a conscious choice, and it is perhaps healthy to let a door close so that a new dawn can arise. Does it serve you to examine how well you are managing the art of living?

Un-conditioning #7 — Fighting the status quo. Begin questioning the way things are. Challenge current practices that no longer serve you on your path. I started to understand that the old structure is being kept alive by those holding on to it, and we don't want it to disintegrate and dismantle because we prefer to stay with what we know and are comfortable with. But in every situation, we are being challenged to make space for action, even in very restrictive circumstances. There was a feeling within me that no longer jibed with where our world was headed, and which had nothing to do with anyone else but the feeling of not letting myself down by not letting my true self emerge. And on this journey, I began to discover the path of least resistance—a place where I didn't need to fight or struggle as I slowly discovered my own balance and peace. It was mostly off the beaten track and in the most unexpected places. That's where my freedom and sovereignty were patiently waiting for me to become aware of what was truly possible.

Our systems are starting to crack and there is opportunity for new bridges to be built to shift into a healthier world. Your opportunity is to relearn how to ask questions like a curious young child instead of blaming, judging, and criticizing, which are all easy to do. You did not come to this planet to suffer. You came here to create. You don't always need traditional goals and ambitions. You can tap into your intuition and trust the currents. Listen to what is being whispered to you, and if you can't hear it, question yourself until the pieces of the puzzle appear as a tapestry. It's some of the hardest and most rewarding work you can ever do.

You may have been conditioned to be liked or to become better than others in a world that celebrates anyone who becomes "someone." Asking questions will most likely allow you to see that you are *already* someone and you don't need to be the "best" in the world when you can choose to become the most authentic version of yourself.

Un-conditioning #8 — There is a veil to reality. Things are not always as they seem. There's something about silence that allows us to hear the vibrations of the universe and become aware. And it starts with each of us doing our own work on healing ourselves and saying "Enough!" to the suffering, the loneliness, the depression, the trauma, the injustice, and all that keeps us terrorized and fearful. Words matter because, when strung together, they become beliefs and vibrations that impact our experiences. We can sit back and watch the news reports of events happening around us, as reported by outside agencies with agendas, and we can also tap into our ability to question to help us step out of being an audience to someone else's agenda.

As someone whose first memory in life is war and missing terrorist attacks by a matter of minutes, I was programmed on the frequency of fearing for my life. I dreamt of peace, and yet there was no peace when the actual fear terrorized me over and over with the vibration of survival and protecting myself from the *bad* people. When I started questioning everything and working toward peace from an early age, I realized we still have work to do within ourselves to heal. And despite the experts telling us how innovative and progressive our world is in the twenty-first century, reality is far from it. Hate is still hate. And despite all the fundraising to eradicate any type of injustice and intolerance for the last few hundred years, we have failed to address the root cause. More and more resources thrown at a problem simply fuels the problem even more. We've been taught to distract ourselves, and our opportunity is to remember how to set boundaries, question, connect, and spark deep dialogue with ourselves and each other. As mentioned already, learning to walk away from toxicity that causes stress in the body and gut is key as we un-condition and learn to walk toward a healthy life filled with possibilities with eyes wide open.

Do you have a feeling that you came here for a reason—beyond having goals and dreams? Do you believe that you've been through enough suffering, loneliness, trauma, and loss? If you ever had an inner knowing that you never fit into the current world, then this may be your time to take action to un-learn and un-condition. And it's no mistake that you've experienced trauma, wounds, and all the suffering that comes along with them. Because it made you strong to be ready for these times of coming face-to-face with yourself.

Questions like "Who are you?" and "What do you want to create?" become incredibly relevant. It's possible to reach a point where you lose sight of who you truly are. You could be prioritizing other people's needs, not feeling fulfilled, or trying to live by what is supposedly good for you or what you should do. Whatever the cause, the loss of purpose can undermine your well-being. But what if you're now in a position to uncover yourself and start doing what feels healthy in your heart? It's a time to "know thyself" and what you are made of and learn how to find your own voice, with integrity, empathy, and courage to be who you are and no longer be more concerned with what people think of you.

Where does your power lie? We were born to live in internal harmony in a healthy body, not being driven to save or fix anyone but ourselves. Change does not happen overnight and requires each of us to be grounded, focused, and see the opportunities around us. The storms will continue to come, but when you can go inside yourself and heal what needs to be healed emotionally and physically, you will be able to be of service, and that's how the tide shifts. That is when the dialogue takes place around what's possible; not creating more sides, more divides where we fight for our life. There are no simple answers, as it's time to really sit with the questions, our imagination, and create the dialogue and healthy structures that can emerge. The experts may spew stuff about collaboration, but we have not touched the surface of what's possible until we engage in real dialogue that fuels creation as our own experts. The rest is just more noise feeding a very conditioned, hungry machine that vies for our attention and consumption.

We experience many beginnings and endings, and in our lifetime we can die over and over. We can learn to let go, transform, and experience rebirth. We can grieve the deaths of our old selves and the deep loss we may experience, but we can also learn to regenerate, rise above, and find our rhythm and vibration to lift ourselves up without fighting for our life. It may go against everything you were conditioned to believe but ultimately you are a powerful being. You no longer have to be a victim or a superhero; you can just be.

You can overcome your conditioning and harness your creative power to align with your highest purpose and potential, to create the world you deserve to live in, one step at a time. For me, this is not just a book but binoculars for your soul—helping you unleash a healthier way of life, a life you are here to enjoy. Some days are tough but the excitement of knowing that we can spark each other keeps me going and keeps the voice whispering to me, never give up. I am dedicating my life to my higher purpose as I continue to un-condition, let go, learn, grow, and create like never before. It is possible.

THE ROAD TO UN-CONDITIONING

Can you spend a few minutes reviewing your own societal conditioning of who and what made you who you are today? How similar or different is it from what was just shared? How does your conditioning relate to your limiting beliefs and where these beliefs originated? What do you feel gets in your way? Are there any areas that you feel keep you stuck in a rut? What are they? Can you tailor them to what is relevant and healthy for you? Now that you have identified your key areas, can you start working on your areas of un-conditioning? Remember that we are each on a journey that is truly as unique as we are.

Are you in any way compromising the integrity of who you are? Are you trying to be what someone else expects you to be? Do you want to be different or do something different, but you find it uncomfortable or risky? Do you have an opportunity to dare to be yourself? Throw caution to the wind, and express yourself in whatever ways feel healthy to you. Can you be a first-rate version of yourself? And if so, who is that person? What are you doing? Take a moment to picture yourself being and doing those things, and then make a mental note of the gap between your imagination and your current reality. What do you need to do to shrink the gap? Do you need courage, faith, a plan, or a change of priority? Is it time to expand, be more adventurous, take a chance, and embrace the possibilities heading your way?

All the money and fame in the world will never give us peace of mind—it will actually drive us to want to consume more and more. Can you be your best self and unlearn what people think is best for you? We'll always be subjected to people who think they know more than we do about what's best for us. It's easy to live in a world where we keep winning or losing, but our true opportunity is to realize everything is here for us to create the life we want and reclaim our imagination of what is possible. No matter how far and wide we seek, no one has our answer—so, do we know what our question is?

When we become self-aware before trying to fix someone else or a broken system, we transform the bigger systems that are cracking. We can first figure out what we want to create while we are here, and then find the other conscious leaders, architects, and organizations who share our desire to create something meaningful in the world with us. We can also decide to practice our art on our own and connect with unexpected and trustworthy partners to create something bigger than ourselves. Sometimes you have to trust the currents in life, even when they lead you in unexpected directions. Take a journey into yourself by better understanding your own conditioning and where your own freedom lies. Is there anything that requires unleashing?

EXPEDITION 4

THE ROAD TO SELF-AWARENESS INCLUDES SELF-LOVE

We were born with brilliant minds and mighty hearts to be creators in this world. Who and what we give our power, energy, and attention to matters deeply. Sometimes it's hard to be in the moment when everything around us is telling us to be productive and efficient every second of our lives.

Many of us have been trained to evaluate every day, every week, every month, and every year by our accomplishments, achievements, failures, and mistakes. Think about the conversation you're having with people at the end of your day—are you reporting on your day? Are you sharing some drama that took place with a friend, spouse, child, parent, coworker, or someone else in your life? What role do events in the world, your community, or your life play in terms of what you bring into your own world? How does your body feel when you think about these conversations? Do they lift you up or bring you down?

One of the ways I learned to walk away from toxic people was to start observing myself. I started becoming aware of my conversations. How often did I invest energy in talking about how badly someone treated me and spend the time venting about them? I started asking myself whether I'd become a victim in their story, and I began considering what type of people I wanted to attract in my life. It took a lot of introspection and experiencing different people to become clear on what was important to me. They were not bad people, but there was no reason to spend energy on finding a path alongside theirs. They showed me who they were more through their actions than their words, and I started paying attention to whether they were in or out of balance with their words and intentions.

I would move on when I felt hurt, instead of pointing fingers or blaming others. I became aware that I am not here to change anyone but myself. My purpose is to be the best version of myself by learning and growing. Over time, I grew increasingly grateful that I was able to learn so much from evaluating the toxicity—understanding when someone was healthy for me and when someone wasn't, and simply moving on. I try my best not to put toxic chemicals on or in my body, and I feel the same way about toxic people. Loving myself means that I don't have to get engulfed in being wronged or not appreciated. It's funny how words don't matter as much to me as how someone shows up consistently.

We can hold our power and define what is safe and scary for us. We can embrace what brings us joy and lifts our spirits just as much as we can embrace what hurts us. We can watch a film or experience a book and venture into the unknown through someone else's story or our own. I met women of all ages, shapes, and sizes in Ubud in

Bali who told me they read *Eat, Pray, Love* and were there to find their true love like author Elizabeth Gilbert did in her story. But every adventure is different, and I hope their trip helped them love themselves more by stepping into the world.

Some people never venture out, believing their view of the world is the only possible one, and it takes courage to face ourselves and be courageous enough to explore our own paths. No two paths or lives, just like leaves on a tree, are ever the same.

Do You Want to Be Famous or Rub Shoulders with Celebrities?

No one really knows. No one has the answers.

People theorize and philosophize, but everyone wants us to believe in their theories and follow their formulas for the *good* life. It's an increasingly noisy and messy world out there right now, and today, many assume that if we "make it big" and are successful, we know how to do "it." But what they don't show us is that while they may have "made it big," they're in a trap, chasing the "good life," numbing themselves with achievements and accomplishments that they were told would make them happy. They rub shoulders and post photos with their successful "tribe" and spend their lives climbing to the top.

No matter how much they try to entice and convince us that they have the answer to reaching nirvana, they don't know us, and we have no idea if what they have is real or an illusion they are selling. And often, it takes curiosity and courage to know ourselves enough to realize that these celebrities and brands would cease to exist if the vast majority of us stopped giving them our attention, money, and power.

Meeting a celebrity may be high on our bucket list, but what if our opportunity is to celebrate ourselves? What if we have enough and *are* enough and don't need to feel worthy by being acknowledged and

validated by rubbing shoulders with celebrities? Our current world ·
will push us to buy into the celebrated experts and authorities, but
the true reality is that no one really knows why we are all here and no
one has our answers. That is the great mystery of life that many are
too scared to explore. And yet, what if we hold the power to unlock
our own worthiness?

Making space in our closet may be important, but making
space in our life can provide many benefits. We are taught about
completion, achievement, and success. It is drilled into us from an
early age to aspire to "become someone." Celebrity and fame are not
only our current currencies but also our sad addictions. When we
take a photo with a well-known person and we post it online, others
want to share in our success of having that moment of glory and
meeting that celebrity in real life. The number of "likes" will spike
like wildfire, and so will jealousy in those who wish that moment
had been captured with them. They too want to be successful and
proud. Who wouldn't want to have a picture taken with Helen Mirren
or LeBron James? But what if we put ourselves in the shoes of that
celebrity, who is a human with insecurities just like anyone else, who
may be thinking about how much she wants to be done with tonight's
photobombs so she can have a cup of tea and stop listening to all the
nonsense around her? Sure, the fame was initially intoxicating, but
now she misses her privacy and the comfort of a few trusted souls to
simply be herself with.

Everyone loves who she portrays on the screen or the stage, and
everyone believes they know her—but very few really do. But once
the stream of fans ends and the camera flashes subside, she can go to
her hotel room and have some peace in being her true self. She knows
the price of fame. Not many want to talk about what happens once
you've made it. A famous musician shared with me that whether you
like it or not, your life radically changes once you become a public

figure. It can be difficult for somebody to connect to you as a human being and not as a celebrity—and yet, you are the same person you have always been.

We are taught about the road to success and to compete with everyone else, apart from ourselves, to be the best we can be. It's always about winning a coveted spot in society. But imagine for a moment that there is a different story available to us, one that is more aligned with who we are and takes us off the universal illusion of success.

For many, this mere thought induces much fear, as there are people who don't want to think for themselves. They would rather follow the prescribed path, as there is a pill for anything we come across to ease our suffering. And that is okay; it's a choice each of us can make. It is our own health that we're responsible for. It is the story that we may choose to adopt as a way of life. We can respect the fact that everyone is doing their best—but never at our own expense. It doesn't mean that we have to follow a certain path that fails to evoke our truth. It takes courage to step out of a story that is no longer—or maybe has never been—serving us.

TAKING A LEAP OF FAITH

By definition, an adventurer is autonomous and an independent thinker, free of society's projections and images. An adventurer develops skills to maneuver the twists and turns of less trodden paths that life throws at us. An adventurer often becomes aware of the traps of a safe life and ventures out at our own pace. It's part of our deep societal conditioning not to question but to accept the lifestyle we were born into. Yet, it is our right to find our voice and discover the paths that are waiting for us to become aware of.

Of course, we cannot snap our fingers and become a professional golf pro, photographer, or chef overnight. But we can become aware of the barrier that is preventing us from taking the first steps toward attaining our calling. When we ignore our irrational fears—such as fearing we are not good enough—and don't allow them to rule us, we find a way to break out and explore the life that is calling to us. We still may not end up being a chef, a professional photographer, or a golf pro, because there is no certainty when we adopt the mindset of an adventurer in the School of Life.

Before embarking on a trip, we plan our itinerary and figure out our route. We may use online maps and input the addresses so we can ascertain how to get there and familiarize ourselves with the local amenities. Most people today use online tools to map out a journey so they know for sure how to get from point A to point B. Yet, in the journey of life, the deeper question to ask ourselves is, "What does my personal navigation system want me to explore?"

When was the last time you decided not to take the fast track or the recommended route and instead chose to listen to your inner guide urging you to take the path that was calling you? When were you brave enough to make the choice that most appealed to you, despite others' objections? Did you enjoy your choice or make another choice until you felt alive and satisfied with your decision? Were you able to do this without guilt or shame?

Is it easy? How can it be, when from an early age we're told by those older and more experienced than us to listen and do what the teacher says? When we were programmed to be good and do our homework and were rewarded for following instructions, we were not taught to question whether these were healthy guidelines for us. We may not have been aware of other choices that were available to us.

This programming was instilled and rooted in our psyche while we were still developing, earning more praise from our parents and we experienced their pride and joy if we excelled more and more at school. It was even compounded as our parents shared our achievements with friends and family. The notion of pride snuck into our life, without us being aware that making someone else proud was part of the overall programming. No wonder as adults we are often scared to think for ourselves. We've been conditioned to feel responsible for our parents' happiness by being good, and terrified of losing their love and appreciation if we do something different and outside the norm. Independence is dangerous and unsafe. What normal person likes danger?

There is an increasing number of us feeling trapped by the status quo, especially when we start seeing the invisible prison walls surrounding us. But can we be held back because of our family and friends' fears? This is our journey, and it's both an exhilarating and a terrifying opportunity to explore our true purpose by becoming increasingly aware of the choices we're making and the possibilities that are available to us. It is always a choice, as Charlotte Brontë reminds us in her book *Jane Eyre*: "I would always rather be happy than dignified."

FACING OURSELVES

People often tell us how to walk toward something or someone, how to attract what we desire into our life—or that we can manifest anything, even a Tesla or Prince Charming in our driveway. Just close your eyes, see it, feel it, breathe it, and that car, that loving relationship, and the good life will magically appear!

The internet is exploding with tips—YouTube videos featuring New Age gurus spewing love and light are now in abundance. I've had people who call themselves *empaths* tell me with certainty what would happen in my life, only for me to find out, when I stopped to listen, how broken their lives were. Though they were truly empathetic, it was up to me to face myself. What I found was that it's about understanding that sending love and light alone doesn't pay our bills—and while having a healthy mindset is important, I found that there is no fast track to manifesting through magical formulas or psychedelic enlightenment. Infusing a substance or a belief rarely leads to nirvana for more than a few hours or days. At some point, we have to get grounded in reality and deal with our shit.

Carl Jung's work about facing our darkness is constantly being brought into the light by many who tell us to kill our egos and move into our hearts. An online search of "the dark night of the soul" could lead one to spending weeks or even months reading all of the theories available on how to deal with our shadows and trauma. While it's necessary to become whole and healthy on the path, it has become trendy, and even a business, for many who may or may not be qualified to help us. And what if instead, we saw an opportunity to become aware of the role our unhealthy ego plays in our life, and then align our healthy ego to our heart? Why is our mind deemed "bad" and our heart "good"?

I delve into this more in the third book of this series, *F*ck the Bucket List for the Health-Conscious: Trusting Our Hearts*, but the bottom line is this: we must all be aware of this trendy, New Age, "love and light" kind of spirituality, which is currently a very big business in the Western world. The "trickster guru" type is never very far away and is always willing to hold our wallets as we face our own "dark night of the soul."

Popular spirituality serves as a way for people to believe we can attract and manifest whatever we want into our lives—but spirituality itself is not a big business, and by its very nature cannot be. There is no quick fix or guru to transform us when we're spiritual. It's up to us to tear down the psychological illusions and beliefs around our self-worth, and examine our beliefs and self-judgment so we can transform. There's no one to blame, protest, or war against when we heal the pieces of ourselves in healthy and integrated ways, and when we dare to come eye-to-eye with our own power source and spirit.

Being spiritual is personal; nobody else knows what makes us tick or how we've been hardwired to be the way we are through our life experiences. We're all here to learn and teach each other along the way. The irony is that most of us have not invested in truly knowing ourselves, and shifting from an unhealthy state of mind (or an unhealthy ego) in balance with our hearts is a way out of this insanity. We've been programmed that more is better in the race to achieve success and fame—but what is it that we actually know deep in our souls? When we are alone and take a long look in the mirror, who is it that we see staring back at us?

Actress Judy Garland advised, "Always be a first-rate version of yourself, instead of a second-rate version of somebody else." What is your best version? Do you remember a time when you were that person, or have you yet to discover your best self? Whether you've lost the essence of who you really are or you've never really known, I encourage you to consider letting your decisions come from a healthy heart that's in alignment with a healthy mind. But to do so, it may be time to face the mirror and see who is looking back at you. It's an opportunity to look at who you are and how you live, and decide how you can best love yourself.

Seeing with Discerning Eyes

The first step is to choose to work on ourselves first. Our world needs healthy living beings. It does not want us to change; it wants to evolve and regenerate. While some systems are healing (literacy, community, agriculture, etc.), others continue to decline (politics, legal, financial, etc.). All one can do is work on oneself, and it's the most rewarding work we can ever do. There is no secret sauce or guru to set us free from our own prisons of the mind. It's the biggest unspoken hoax available to each of us.

Imagine, once again, if we taught kids from a young age to discern what's healthy for them and what's not for them so they could create their own beautiful path rather than have to be placed in someone else's boxes of success. But so many parents today are wounded ourselves, and there is a need for massive healing on this planet. Imagine what would happen if we inspired our kids through action, not just words. A parent who practices self-care and self-love is an amazing teacher.

It's only when we realize how truly powerful we are that we can recognize that we've been gifted the power to make choices. Choices in what we want to walk toward and choices in when, who, and what we want to walk away from (and sometimes actually run). So, ask yourself:

- What and who am I walking toward with curiosity and awe? Why?
- Who am I attracting into my life, and why?
- How is it aligned to who I am at my core? Why or why not?
- Tell a story about the people in your life, and tie self-love into it.

These questions can help you know what and who is not for you. Please add your own questions to the mix, as only you know what to ask yourself. This is just to help spark the fire in you to face what's deep inside.

Then, ask yourself something like this:

- What people, beliefs, stories, and ideas are no longer serving me? Have they ever? Why?

- Why am I still in these stories? What's holding me there? What role am I playing?
- Do I want to stay in these situations and stories? What would happen if I were to walk away?
- What does walking away mean to me? Is it something I have the capability to do now, or later? Is it something I feel I can do? What support system do I need, if any, to take a leap of faith, and why?

These questions may help you to understand what's unhealthy for you and is weighing on your soul. What questions will help you? What support do you truly need?

You may find yourself moving deeper and deeper into the unknown, questioning beliefs that you may not have realized you held—everything from the physical world you were born into to questions about who you really are. And in this process of awakening to who you are, you'll come across false beliefs and shackles that have held you back from living a healthy life—a life where you can experience the world through a healthy state of mind that thrives on knowing your true purpose and what gives you meaning. It will guide you on how to relate to your body, nature, society, and everyone you come across, and help you face any highs and lows that are thrown at you with wonder, compassion, and even joy. But like any great adventure that may start off frightening at the outset, it can become enriching with curiosity, hard work, courage, and staying the course. There's no map to follow as you set your rhythm at your own pace. And don't be discouraged if your old ways return; it's always an opportunity to learn. Unhealthy habits can have a strong hold on you and take time and compassion to break free from.

I fire myself often from different situations when I discover the emerging stories are not for me and not aligned to who I'm becoming.

People around me often think I'm crazy for walking away from what they see as amazing opportunities and very successful people, and that's okay. I have been brought up to think about what is right or wrong, what is good or bad, what is appropriate or inappropriate. I now choose to ask different questions that are more aligned with my core: is this person, organization, belief, story, food, situation, system healthy or unhealthy for me? Is it for me or not for me? There's no one else on this planet who can answer this question for me.

Much changes when we realize how powerful we are and that the choices we can make matter deeply. Our internal compass is available when we're ready to navigate our life in a healthy direction, at our own time and our own pace. I've guided people to cross their invisible bars and try many things until they uncovered their own sovereignty and tapped into their ability to be in their power. To go from the need to be heard to unleashing their true voice. There's really nothing more rewarding.

Making Friends with Fear

Feel into your fear, but don't cultivate irrational fear. Becoming aware of the difference between rational and irrational fear is the first step. Rational fear is one of the necessities of basic human survival. It will help protect us from touching a hot stove, walking into oncoming traffic on a busy street, and avoiding a black bear in the yard. Irrational fear is the perceived fear inside our heads that has been inculcated since childhood by family, friends, teachers, and other authority figures and that produced the recording "you are not good enough" or "you don't have enough."

Fear has been instilled into many by influential cultural backgrounds, as well as grandparents and parents passing it along to their offspring. It's an unspoken epidemic that many want to release but don't know how. How can we release our fears? By becoming aware that fear is the best-selling brand in our world and it's spreading like wildfire. Societal programming wants us to fear so we'll consume more. Isn't it insane that companies call us consumers and see us as their "audience"? It's us who feed their growth through the choices we make.

Some people are learning to step out of our mental prisons—and you, too, may be yearning to break free. But that feeling of freedom, which is totally unknown after so many years in captivity, can be scary—just as a wild animal that has adapted to being taken care of while being nursed back to health is very unsure and fearful of being set free after months of rehabilitation. The open plains or the majestic mountains are very daunting. The uncertainty of being able to find its flock or herd, or anxiety about how it will survive when it crosses the invisible line from its confinement, fills it with fear. Ultimately, however, its instincts kick in and it runs toward freedom.

When you look at nature, you see that change happens constantly as the animal and plant kingdoms interact every second. It's a natural process that humans try to manage and control. For example, think about the billions of dollars that have poured into parts of the world for humanitarian aid during our lifetime. The fact that safe water continues to be a scarce commodity, one in five kids goes to bed hungry in America, and disease and suffering is still very prevalent on our planet doesn't seem to be addressed. It's not something that can be eradicated by writing a check every year. Yes, it helps, but it does not yield sustaining and lasting results.

It's estimated that there are approximately ten million nonprofit organizations worldwide operating in the humanitarian sector, and yet the numbers related to hunger, disease, and homelessness are still staggering. Saving the world has become a lucrative business in a world where no one wants to be truly saved or fixed. How can we accept living in a state of division, fear, or war when we know how sacred life is?

Self-Awareness Is One of the Most Important Skills of Our Time

We can go deeper. It begins with the self—me, myself, and I. Change can only start on an individual level, not with the need to change someone else or the world. Why? Because life is changing every second of every day, and we are the point of reference from which our life force flows. Nature is one of our biggest teachers, and yet many have simply forgotten that change is an element of life, not something to be managed or controlled. We can learn to adapt and change to make a difference in our lives and in our communities.

No one wants to be saved or fixed, and yet that is what we practice and teach. The hardest work you will ever do starts with self-examination. No robot, software program, or app will be able to take on this task for you. The buck stops with you!

When you stop warring within yourself, you'll have a healthier vantage point to then step out into the world to create healthier systems that take into account every living being on the planet. When you stop consuming unhealthy beliefs and products, you'll be able to create healthy paths with other pioneers who want to co-create a healthier world.

More and more people are seeking more meaning in our lives. The material things no longer seem enough to satisfy or bring lasting happiness. How many people wake up every day and sit in traffic to arrive at a job that does not fulfill us? All because we need to pay our bills and feed our families. Was this the purpose—to raise kids to be held hostage by duties and obligations so we can be labeled as responsible adults?

We are the captain of our own ship. And the storms are natural;

there's no denying they'll come into our path at some point. The amusement parks that we've constructed have roller coasters that allow us to experience highs and lows as we take twists and turns on their course. We can get on and off a rollercoaster as much as we choose—but we can't deny the storms when they arrive at our ships, and they will. Those storms often appear as stories in the form of a comedy, thriller, tragedy, horror, or drama.

Seeking the Next High

There are many unspoken addictions and invisible bars all around us in our society today. One of the most prevalent is participating in someone else's drama. We're constantly fed the excitement through television shows, news media, film, and social media platforms. Why? Because it sells by feeding our adrenaline, which makes us feel alive. It connects us with other human beings as we interact to share the thrill. Yet, how many of us pause and consider what this does to us as individuals and to our lives?

It becomes an addiction. There is a constant yearning for more to feed the high and the exhilaration. The body reacts the same, whether it is fear or excitement being experienced. Next time you watch a tragedy on the news or a thrilling sports feat, notice whether there is any difference in your emotional body. Is there any contrast in the sensations?

As with any addict, the focus becomes the need to find the next high, the opportunity to share our own personal dramas with whoever is willing to engage. Yes, the stories meet our need to vent and be heard, but they also provide the high as we relive the incident or event. Notice also how our stories become more embellished as we go deeper into how we were wronged or the need to blame someone else for our circumstances.

Addiction is addiction when we find ourselves rehashing and retelling the stories we're stuck in, spinning more and more by the injustice of it all. It does not matter if it's coming from the outside world or from our personal lives. There is no difference. What matters is that we take responsibility for our lives in a way that works for us by becoming aware of when we are in one of these cycles. And yes, it takes practice to be fully aware of whether we're starting, directing, or writing the drama. We can teach ourselves to stop the cycles of drama, blame, and judgment. We can cease looking for meaning in drama and find a new meaning that invigorates us. Life becomes purposeful, and "high on life" will take on a whole new direction.

Every thought, every action, and every reaction matters more than we can imagine. Within each moment, we hold immense power to change our situation, not solely by what we do, but through who we're becoming. There is no magic bullet or how-to guide that provides us with our answers. It's the School of Life that we can play with when we're ready to go on the most exhilarating journey of discovery. When was the last time, or the first time, you commended yourself on what an amazing job you're doing navigating your life?

When Rules and Lists Work Against Us

Rules and regulations are a necessity to create some kind of order for dealing with the masses. Like everything, they are set up for the good, but are not effective when they become rigid and inflexible to the point of being confining. Of course, there are some who find comfort in them, but too many restrictions can be counterproductive for our evolution. It's healthy to understand these rules so we can break them down and see where they are hindering our creativity and expansion.

A government agency sent me a letter instructing me on how they wanted to deal with an issue their process uncovered. Instead of being pissed off or complaining, I contacted them and told them that I'd like to find another way to resolve the issue they flagged. Luckily, I found an incredibly reasonable human being and we worked through everything. The bottom line was that they didn't force me to comply, which was shocking in itself. But I realized that it was time to stand within my power and challenge rules that didn't make sense. When you prefer to carefully color within the lines of conformity, you may find that you respond positively to strong rules, which maintain order and create the illusion of safety—but please consider that it may prevent you from exploring anything beyond the norm and outside of what is expected to live a successful life.

Many times, rules and lists become unnecessary walls that prevent us from living up to our full potential. Our societal code traps us in acceptable norms that are really no more than rules of how we should interact with the world. I know firsthand that there is so much more, and these rules can be very stifling, especially when it comes to our creativity and imagination. Sure, we all need guidelines and signposts to help us navigate, but we can also practice questioning everything in order to invite in more common sense that seems to be dwindling in today's climate. We've been gifted beautiful minds and hearts to explore the edges and question the boundaries. This is where the fun begins as we approach them with curiosity and a sense of play.

Rules keep us in a very structured, black-and-white world—but we need to be more aware of exceptions, because life is not black and white. We can be more flexible and open to these exceptions, as there are many shades of gray in the world. Rules tend to push us into confined, polarized boxes.

History is a great teacher—and it repeats itself, over and over again, so we know what happens when people follow blindly. When we're able to see these patterns, there is an opportunity to break out of the cycles that no longer serve. Too many rules allow people to hide and become complacent. Is it really healthy to live in a world of followers who do not question? We desire some semblance of order, but what happens when it becomes counterproductive and the very same rules work against us?

Stepping Out of Conformity

The bottom line is that many of us are afraid of our thoughts and questions. It's easy to go from one activity to another activity, complete one task and move to the next, put items on a bucket list, make plans, and follow someone else's rules. For myself, I found it easy to pick up a book that outlined how to achieve success but had a hard time adopting someone else's generic process of how to be successful or manifest nirvana. And whether it was a book, a workshop, or a lecture, I never fit into someone else's model and loved the freedom of experimenting instead of following guidelines or rules. In the pursuit of meaning, there is magic in recognizing the value in pausing to think—and now, more than ever, being mindful allows us to have a healthier understanding of ourselves.

Very few want to think about doing something differently when the rules work against us. It's more fun and fulfilling to gather and connect with others, and complain about how unjust and unfair the rules are. It's not really socially acceptable to question current rules and structures, and it actually scares the hell out of a lot of people. It's much simpler to blame others, or to follow experts that claim they have the answers without practicing what they preach. Would you rather live in a world with healthy dialogue, respecting many voices and perspectives, than one filled with preaching and manipulation?

At one point in my career, I worked for one of the leading change management gurus in the world, whose books and methodologies were best sellers. I experienced firsthand that while he got into the highest levels of business, his words did not match his actions. He had the tools to teach others how to change and work together, but inside the walls of his organization, his wrath would erupt if he was ever questioned. He was the almighty knowing source, and you were told how lucky you were to have a job at his company. I didn't stay there very long, but I remain grateful to have had a front row seat in viewing the insanity of it all.

It's much easier to come up with reasons why we can't change the rules or our beliefs than it is to question them. Many simply unconsciously choose to suffer. We tend to shun what we don't understand, what we don't like, and become very judgmental as a form of protection to avoid dealing with our fears and seeing our opportunities.

Becoming Aware of the Traps

It can be a trap to live our lives through a detailed plan with bucket lists, which has us focused on arriving at specific destinations. When we work on projects, they usually have defined goals, deliverables, timelines, and metrics. Should our lives have this same framework? In 1932, at a New Jersey Education Association meeting, Albert Einstein wisely shared, "The school of life is chaotic and plan-less, while the school system operates according to a definite plan."

Our opportunity is not to wait for someday, treading water until the perfect time arrives to blaze our trails to explore opportunities. The downside of a concrete plan is that it doesn't leave much room for the imagination. It tends to be rigid and doesn't allow for fun detours or surprises. When we have such a fundamental map worked out in our minds for our lives, we may never embark on our paths.

Instead of feeling overwhelmed by how big our plans are, how many items are left to achieve on our bucket lists, or how much we're setting out to accomplish in our careers, consider a smaller step. The decision at hand is not whether we can get to our destination or not—it's much simpler. It's a choice of whether we'll *start* or not.

Many people, when planning a vacation—and even our life, in some cases—feel more comfortable having an itinerary from the time we leave the first port until the end of the trip. My father worked in the airline and tourism industries and was a lover of knowledge. When I was a child, I traveled the world with my parents whenever the opportunity presented itself. I found myself, from a young age, in a world where there was a plan for everything. Every minute of the trip was filled with museum visits, tours, and activities. You may think I was lucky, and I probably was—but as I got older, I found the itineraries to be confining and felt boxed in by them. I wanted to discover the unexpected gems, get lost, explore unusual places, and meet local people to share stories and hear about other lifestyles.

Of course, it's a very personal choice to want to know ourselves well enough to understand what sparks and ignites our soul. Observing the signposts along the way matters, and letting them guide us so we're constantly pushing the boundaries to expand our experiences to the fullest extent allows us to live on our terms.

WHY PUT LIFE ON HOLD FOR SOMEDAY?

You can start walking and feeling into the flow of life. Simply begin by listening to your intuition, and put the predetermined map down. None of us can ever know where the trail will lead, but we can be willing to be open to unexpected surprises along the way. You will probably be disappointed at times, but it can make you appreciate the unexpected discoveries even more. There will always be reasons why you can't do certain things; it is much harder to shift your mindset to start considering why, and how, you can. What if you become fully aware of what truly sparks and ignites you, and not put it on a *someday* bucket list that defines your ultimate destination? What are the things, now that you know what's healthy for you, that you *cannot not* do? For me, I was conditioned to give my power away and to feel that someone else had my answers; it was time to step into my power by trekking into the unknown. I took small steps and learned to flow through the lessons that showed up on my path by trusting the universe.

Please be careful with bucket lists; they have a tendency to be another box that can trap us with the burden of preconceived accomplishments that one day we hope to tick off our list before we die. Too many people fall into a trap and bring along things and people they don't really need or want in our lives.

Our adventure is one for the soul. We're explorers experiencing life by putting ourselves out there and living in possibilities. Society offers us perceived safety and hazard zones, which keeps us in boxes, too often scared to venture into the unknown.

Traveling and exploring is for the soul, while a bucket list is for the mind. Short-term goals are beneficial to guide us to the next point and still allow us to experience the reality of life as it shows up in the moment. It takes courage to make decisions and choices. Consider that our true job may be to find the courage to open up uncharted paths. We can then decide if it is healthy for us, or stay where we are until something else opens up.

If this seems terrifying to you, find out why and have a conversation with yourself about what safety and danger mean to you. Of course, I am not suggesting you jump out of a plane without a parachute or punch a tiger in the nose. However, please ask yourself questions that will help you understand yourself better. You can choose to do things now and fill your life with purposeful adventures instead of wishful bucket lists that may lose their meaning or value someday in the future. And why put your life on hold if it's something within your reach? The person with the most possessions and items ticked off their list is not necessarily the "winner" of a beautiful life.

The End or the Beginning?

When we venture out to the end of Highway 101, we'll find ourselves in Canada, on a two-lane highway in a small town called Lund in British Columbia. The history of the town from the 1960s has been documented in a film called *The End of the Road*. The locals will tell us that this is where the highway begins, while those who travel regularly on this highway in the United States believe it is where it ends. Being adventurous can yield different experiences, especially when you start facing your relationship with the unknown. Life and death are cycles in life; just like endings and beginnings or beginnings and endings.

We are living in a cultural moment where we may find ourselves very busy getting to where we believe we need to be at every moment of the day. There is more traffic on the roads than ever before—from two lanes to as many as six lanes in some big urban areas. There are more choices and options now than ever before on how to navigate your journey to reach your destination. Too often in life, we settle for the one lane that we have been told is safe and will lead us to a full life. Even though we know there are other lanes and different routes, it's too scary to try something new. Do you know what, if anything, is stopping you from driving in a different lane or taking the scenic route?

Unlike with most jails, being stuck in life does not have guards or physical bars to keep you imprisoned. The only person who can release you, or give you parole, is you. Luckily, you're not in a physical jail, so you don't have to ask anyone for permission to be free. Are you in touch with your imagination, courage, and boldness for action? What's your deeper purpose? Why are you here? Can you propel yourself toward new horizons and find a way out of the insane rat race that humanity has constructed?

Author Brené Brown has been on the road to self-love: "I now see how owning our story and loving ourselves through that process is the bravest thing that we'll ever do."

EXPEDITION 5

EVERY MOMENT IS A FRESH BEGINNING

Wherever we go, we'll most likely attract the same type of people, whether locally or across the globe, because it's we who are the magnet. Regardless of where we are, we'll be drawing in the same people, having the same conversations, and seeking the same experiences in the hopes of bumping into something different. We'll still be seeking something outside of ourselves—or maybe an answer or secret we believe someone else holds.

There are many temptations that come into our paths with people trying to sell us on their way of life. It starts early on—in school, for example, where students experience divisions of who is accepted and popular. Those who are rejected are told they aren't cool enough to be part of the popular clique. This is embedded in every society ever created, cultivating the desire to become someone others are proud of at an extremely early, influential age. But as we mature, we realize that it's more about connecting deeply with ourselves that truly ignites us in ways we never imagined.

In his book *Fahrenheit 451*, author Ray Bradbury writes, "Everyone must leave something behind when he dies, my grandfather said. A child or a book or a painting or a house or a wall built or a pair of shoes made. Or a garden planted. Something your hand touched some way so your soul has somewhere to go when you die, and when people look at that tree or that flower you planted, you're there.

"It doesn't matter what you do, he said, so long as you change something from the way it was before you touched it into something that's like you after you take your hands away. The difference between the man who just cuts lawns and a real gardener is in the touching, he said. The lawn-cutter might just as well not have been there at all; the gardener will be there a lifetime."

When walking one day at a local bazaar in Quito, Ecuador, after we returned from the Amazon, I ran into one of the women, who was looking for special items that would be the center of conversation when she got back home. The adventure we experienced in the rain forest was not enough for Ellen; everything seemed to be about needing material things to take up the broken space inside her. The penny dropped—we don't need trinkets or props; people who are ready will show up. Just like the Buddhist teaching says, "when the student is ready, the teacher will appear." There is no need to travel so far to uncover what is already here inside of us. But we might need to take that trip or attend that conference or event to truly see and understand this.

AN EYE FOR AN EYE SIMPLY
KEEPS US BLINDLY DIVIDED

At a breakfast conversation at a conference I was speaking at, a woman was adamant that she and her husband would not be attending his childhood friend's wedding because the couple supported a different political party than they did. Annie was allowing her husband to attend his friend's bachelor party but not the wedding, because she couldn't imagine interacting with people who were aligned to the other political party. Their friendship seemed to be tested by who was in power in their country.

Our divisions are getting wider and more dogmatic. The more we refuse to mingle outside of our social circles, the more we'll continue to stay stuck in the same belief systems and build the same ineffective infrastructure and unhealthy blueprint models. It will be simply experiencing the same reality over and over again, just like the film *Groundhog Day,* where Bill Murray plays Phil, a bitter and self-centered television weatherman who is sent with his producer Rita and cameraman Larry to the annual Groundhog Day festivities in Pennsylvania.

The locals await the appearance of Punxsutawney Phil, the groundhog who will determine the length of winter by his ability to see his own shadow. A freak snowstorm strands all of them in Punxsutawney, and Phil wakes up the next morning with the strangest sense of déjà vu: he seems to be living February 2, 1992, over and over again. No matter what he tries—from imprisonment, to attempted suicide, to kidnapping the groundhog—he relives the same day. This bizarre situation he finds himself in forces him to pause and take an interest in the people around him. He tries to save the life of a homeless man, and then he falls in love with Rita and wants to be someone she could love in return.

One of our biggest opportunities is to truly *see*, maybe for the first time in our lives. To stop and see is a gift when we perceive the world through healthy eyes and thoughts. Our current world is structured in division, separation, and fragmentation. Can we see now what happens when situations are designed for these deep divisions, where we can either be a winner or a loser? For one team or one person to win, the other must lose. That is how the current game is played. Everyone is a "warrior" today in their battles, their adversaries, their camps—spreading more fear, greater division, more anger, and more pain, making us all a little bit blind. We teach our kids to win at all costs and to be the best in the world, often at their own expense.

Some days it is so hard to know what is real and what is false with all the information we have access to today. For many of us, it can get to be too much at times to be asked to distinguish between the two and also be expected to solve the problems of our deeply divided world. The question many are starting to wrestle with is, can we let go of being right or wrong, or judging people as wrong when they don't agree with us? I have stopped trying to correct people or convince anyone of anything. Why would I want to do anyone's work for them?

Sometimes, when I have a front-row seat where two people are arguing and need to be right and win, I feel this unbelievable sadness in my body. I envision them as hurt six-year-olds throwing sand in each other's eyes. And when I've reflected on it, I've become aware that what made me sad is that I saw they had so much in common and if they put down their swords, they could be connecting around something they cared about, instead of participating in a power struggle. And when I can, I try to bring them back to have a conversation and stop needing to overpower each other, which is how we've been hardwired through our parents and societal conditioning.

Much depends on our ability to break cycles or any negative patterning. We have an opportunity to create our own space for connecting with our internal peace and not get dragged into something that could potentially be draining. When we have family or friends that don't see eye to eye with us, it could be very challenging to have to deal with and stay our course. Many of us have unresolved anger or fear that can appear at any moment. Our response and reaction depends on how conscious and mindful we are.

When we choose to stop trying to fix others, we have a greater ability to connect with no expectations or agendas. No one really wants to be saved or fixed—we want to explore and learn for ourselves. It's easier to focus on fixing someone else than fixing ourselves. It's easy to want to change the world instead of ourselves. We're taught to strive for peace, but peace is peace. As Mahatma Gandhi tried to share with us, "There is no 'way to peace,' there is only 'peace.'" There is nothing to strive for, and yet in the striving we download fear daily, which is freely distributed to those who want their next fix.

As soon as we reclaim our power and see what promises we want to fulfill, we can help ourselves and the world. When we integrate peace into our personal lives, it starts to flow into a collective experience. Imagine what can happen when we integrate ourselves and stop warring; would we be able to build healthy learning centers and regenerative agriculture and clean up our environment, for example? I hope that we find our resilience to keep these kinds of inspired actions moving forward. We need the courage to see everything that is happening on our planet holistically, weaving together like a tapestry of unity. Each one of us has come here with a role and we're becoming increasingly aware of why we're here. This is one way we can step out of the need to win and into our deep meaningful mission. There are many voices of change in the world and our power comes together when we shift to creation without the need to fight. Ask yourself, "What role did I come here to play?"

Dr. Natalie Leigh Dyer is a woman of great action and inspiration.

As a neuroscientist and energy healer, she integrates the scientific and the mystical. As a scientist, Natalie studies the power of mind–body medicine and spirituality for wellness, healing, and prevention of illness and disease. As the president of the Center for Reiki Research, Natalie focuses on the benefits of Reiki on physical and psychological health, and shares the teachings on using scientific inquiry to bring us back in balance. A study published in the *Journal of Alternative and Complementary Medicine* in 2019 found that a single session of Reiki improves multiple variables that are related to both physical and psychological health. For more details on the study, you can look into that specific publication.

At Harvard University, Natalie ran many studies. A study on the nocebo effect and the common cold found that the common cold is caused by thousands of different viruses—including rhinoviruses and coronaviruses. Dr. Dyer and her team took saliva samples and told half the subjects that their saliva showed they were developing a cold. About a third of the nocebo group went on to actually develop a cold, while the other group showed no difference. Their immune response (IgA levels) was affected right after the false diagnosis. Dr. Dyer hypothesizes that the stress about developing a cold caused this response and increased their likelihood of actually developing a cold. Her findings show how important our belief system and mindset is to our overall health.

At the International Symposium for Contemplative Studies in San Diego in 2016, Dr. Dyer along with F. Pagnini, C. Park, B. Davoodia, and E. J. Langer presented their research titled *Mindsets Contribute to Changes in Common Cold Symptomatology and Immune Function*. Their main observation was that "these types of studies are very rare because they can harm participants. Because of this we have no idea the true extent of the nocebo effect, and probably never will." What they did observe was how powerful our minds truly are.

Any kind of breakdown—in the body, society, home, work, or a relationship—begins with separation and division. For example, in the body, if there's a lack of cohesion and an inability for every part to work together and function as a whole, it leads to disease and illness. We're being called to discover our wholeness and build up our immunity—not just within our home and society but also within our bodies. What do you need to do to bring yourself together and become a united front? As you strive to create wholeness within yourself, your strength will ripple out into other areas of your life, creating a much stronger foundation from which to ground and integrate yourself.

WHAT'S DRIVING YOU?

Words carry a lot of weight, but it's only through our actions that we bring true clarity and ideas to life. When our words are not matching up with the vibration of what we're doing, we're only disrespecting and harming ourselves.

Talk is cheap, as they say. It's easy to talk about intentions and purpose, but it takes a lot more energy, courage, and effort to take steps to make them real. When we continue to only talk about them, with no action, we slowly lose faith in ourselves. Without action, we're not backing up our words and are literally demonstrating to ourselves that we don't believe in our ability to create. We can get stuck in a theory or philosophy, and it becomes a trap and a form of self-sabotage. It's like having a colleague offer to bring coffee in the morning, only to still be waiting a week later for them to show up with the coffee. We would lose faith in their promises and remain leery, suspended in the never-ending promise of potential.

When we examine our actions, we can ask ourselves whether we're following through on our words. Are they aligned? For example, we may express concern about inequality in the world (the problem), but what small steps are we taking to shift the concern to action that moves away from outrage and more division to create what we envision for how we can live in harmony (the opportunity)? When we no longer need to talk or fight against inequality is when it will become part of this reality, because we would have created a much-needed path toward unity by giving attention to creating the path, rather than fighting the current problem. This applies universally.

Our sovereignty lies in our awareness and willingness to create a life that is free of restrictions, divisions, and limitations. This doesn't mean that awareness on its own will shift us out of existing paradigms, but it's a very significant first step to understanding whether we're creating more suffering in our lives or creating joy through unity. We have a history of focusing on and dissecting what's holding us back—staying in this story of separation and hate, over and over again.

It doesn't matter who is telling this story, what countries these characters reside in, or the plot. The real question is, how ready and able are we to write our own stories? There is no one coming to save us, so we don't really have to wait much longer for a wild transformation to take place. It won't be ushered in with the same mindsets and solutions that have made up the unhealthy parts of the world that created win–lose paradigms, mostly because we're trekking into the unknown. It requires each of us to commit to what we want to truly create, without putting ourselves on hold, and bringing holistic thinking with us. We may need to pause, but we can also simply decide to get in touch with our own voice and create possibilities. There are billions of intersecting paths for us to explore when we're ready for the adventure of a lifetime.

It takes effort to observe what we talk about, listen to, and who we say we are—and even more effort to examine *why* we're doing what we are doing. It's easy to criticize and throw stones. It takes courage to take action and live our purpose. It's important to notice when our actions don't align with our philosophy, and to consider how to best change our words so they reflect the way we show up in life. The clearer we are in expressing our truth to ourselves, the more power we will find in living our true purpose and experiencing life.

When we adopt a mindset where we see possibilities and take action, much can happen. A whole plethora of possibilities opens up! For example, take a moment to imagine that everything is possible. Use your imagination to see and sense blockages melting away and your imagination turning into a reality. Now, feel yourself still grounded, sitting in your chair, and realize that it does take clarity, discipline, and a lot of creativity to make it real. Yes, your life can change and be different—the possibilities are endless. The question to ask is, what role are you willing to play to shift the elements? What's in your way? What bridges will you need to construct and create? Do you get defensive when your fundamental beliefs are challenged? What unhealthy practices, beliefs, and people will you need to address to walk down healthy pathways?

Many of us live largely on the mental plane, but if we spend too much time there, we could easily think our life away. The antidote to all this thinking, analysis, and possible information overload is to play. For me, much shifted when I started to consider how I could have more fun in my life and have a more playful relationship with knowledge, in my own way. So, I ask you, what do you enjoy? What would you love to do more of? What do you imagine that lights you up? Can you imagine something small that will lift your spirits? Poet Mary Oliver asks, "Tell me, what is it you plan to do with your one wild and precious life?"

Do You Dare to Create?

We each have been given a manual of how life is supposed to be, based on our upbringing and culture. What might happen if we knew we had the power to rewrite or edit the manual for our own personal use? Do we want to put it on a list and cross it off someday, or do we want to reimagine it within our current reality?

It's understandable why people put things on hold, but the moment is now. The power is in this moment. Think about it. Use this moment to ask yourself why you are putting off a decision or putting your life on hold. Your life is happening *right now,* as you experience this book. This is your own experience, at this moment, as you read or listen. Take a few minutes and imagine you woke up one day and changed your narrative. What if you asked yourself, for example, "How am I treating life?" instead of, "How is life treating me?" Who would be in the driver's seat in this scenario? Who would be the navigator and the creator? Where does your power lie? Where do you imagine it being sparked and ignited?

When we can recognize how fortunate we are to have important lessons early on in our lives, we may be able to put down someone else's well-used map so we can navigate with our own navigation system. It's not easy for most of us, including me, to create balance in our lives.

We've been brought up with the illusion that there is an ultimate goal, a destination, a sign to wait for. But what if I told you that we can program our own operating system to discover our own path in a noisy, divided world? What if we shifted from believing what we were told was good for us to what is healthy for us? What stuff would we truly need? What food would we be consuming? What thoughts would we feed our mind? What types of people would we surround ourselves with, and who would we invite into our hearts?

Think of yourself as an adventurer who loves to experiment. Someone who has to set off on a mysterious, previously untrodden path that will lead into uncharted territory. Don't worry whether you have a map and directions; you have an internal compass, and it's called your intuition.

TAKING THE FIRST STEPS

At a deeper level, what we may need to consider is whether we're being true to what we value. If not, why are we not being authentic? Joy often has little to do with how much money and security we have, and more to do with whether we honor what we believe by living a meaningful life.

It often feels safer to stay where we are and to continue to believe what we believe. When we don't think change is possible, we don't have to try or do anything to make it possible. We can just agree that it's not possible and blame the lack of change on others. In doing so, we decide to continue on the path that keeps us comfortable and we may wonder why we feel stuck.

For many people, the value of one's imagination has been demeaned and devalued. Twenty-year-old German student Max Planck decided that he wanted to study physics at the University of Munich. His professor told him that everything in that field had already been discovered and that all that remained for him to do was to fill a few unimportant holes and gaps in the literature. The professor tried to convince him to take another path. Max was not only a scientist, he was also a dreamer who ignored this expert advice and ended up winning a Nobel Prize in physics in 1918 for formulating quantum theory.

People will try to convince us that they have our answer, but we can learn to listen to our intuition and make our own choices instead of living someone else's story. Wisdom from Max Planck, one of the top physicists of our time, suggests that "science cannot solve the ultimate mystery of nature. And that is because, in the last analysis, we ourselves are a part of the mystery that we are trying to solve."

When we are automatically sure we have what we need, and we're unaware that we're operating on a default setting, then we probably won't reimagine anything that is unknown or mysterious. But if we really want to explore and create possibilities, then we're aware that there may be another way. We can rediscover and create a healthy relationship with nature, one that likely will emerge from our imagination, self-compassion, and courage to walk our own path.

Do You See Problems or Opportunities?

Nobody leads a charmed life for very long, even if it looks that way on the surface. Everyone has, to some degree, a difficulty—a lesson to learn or a hurdle to leap. While a family of four living in their car or on the streets has issues of daily survival, some of the wealthiest people in the world who have multiple homes and jets have their own demons to face. And sure, we're not comparing their circumstances at all when it comes to adversity. But each one of us is facing ourselves and our situations. What we have in common is our inability to understand the magnitude of each other's daily problems.

When we realize that we are here to birth our own life and not compete to be the best in the world or take anyone down, we can tap into our creativity and determination. Can you see your opportunities as much as you can see your problems and challenges? Your attitude and mindset count for more than you know—so the question is, can you make lemonade out of lemons, or can you only taste the sourness in your lemons?

It is far saner to focus on the opportunity instead of being stuck in the pattern of trying to fix a problem while working from the same assumptions, and within the same system, that created the so-called problem in the first place. I'm not saying you need to ignore your problems. I'm saying that when you recognize a problem, you shouldn't simply try to "fix" it, but rather allow this crack to show you potentially healthier opportunities that you may not have otherwise seen.

You can begin by catching yourself every time you start a thought with "The problem is . . ." or "The trouble is . . ." and see if you can tap into what the *opportunity* is instead. Like any learning you commit to, it takes time, patience, self-compassion, and effort to master healthy habits and mindsets. You've got to stick to it and not give up just because you feel you are not moving forward fast enough. You are on a journey to relearn what is healthy and unhealthy for you—only *you* can redefine what that means and truly own it.

Peter Benchley wrote the best-selling book *Jaws*, which later became an iconic movie. It's the story of a great white shark that stalks and kills people in a small beach town. Later in his life, Benchley deeply regretted the fear the movie generated, which led to human predation of sharks and steep drops in shark populations. To atone, he became an advocate for shark conservation. If there's anything you regret, you can learn from your mistakes, make up for your lack of awareness, and change your habits to balance a time when you acted unconsciously. One of your opportunities is to learn to be present and find your path of least resistance.

Reconsider What Being Lost Means to You

Is it always a bad thing to be lost? To wander into the unknown without a map or a destination? I'd like to propose a healthy version of being lost. It asks that we're willing to let go of our certainties and absolutes. It requires us to question the beliefs that have structured our world and observe them with compassion and curiosity. We don't need to show up as the fearless hero validated by others with superpowers. Rather, we trust that life provides blessings and lessons that were not possible until we allowed ourselves to simply get lost. Can you imagine the best thing that can happen when you take what society calls a "wrong turn"?

What I learned firsthand, through trial and error on my path, is that the people who are truly creating a healthier world—which is quietly emerging—do not list "shifting consciousness" as one of their five superpowers. They're not telling us how we should live our lives and do not live in blame, judgment, or shame. How can anyone have our answers when there is no road map to where we're headed? The current world is noisy, and so many are vying for our attention that it can quickly become overwhelming. There are so many people I've come across who think they have the answer to a good life or a better world, and yet beyond their words and convictions, there is vast emptiness and much trauma.

I have seen some stand in front of a room wanting to serve as a teacher without doing their own work first. Only when we spend time with people outside the "classroom" will we discover how authentic they truly are—because in real life, there is no place to hide. The more time I spent with people who were truly unhealthy for me, the more I appreciated life giving me the opportunity to get closer to its simplicity. I no longer invested as much time and energy in pointing out the flaws of others or the injustice of my situation. Instead, I voted them off my island and kept creating at my own pace with a deep knowing that I was much healthier on my own than when perpetuating a history of suffering. I was more focused on addressing how I was hurting and disappointing myself than being a victim in someone else's story.

It helped me see that most of us simply want dignity and to be seen as we are, not molded and changed into someone else's definitions. It's only when I began my own journey and became conscious of who and what I was letting into my life that I understood who I wanted to play with in this abundant world of opportunities.

We don't need to get lost in someone else's dream or wait for someone else to discover the beauty within us. We've been conditioned to seek others for their knowledge and wisdom, often at our own expense. I needed to step off the path I was told to follow and find my own way. I had to become my own best friend and trust myself before bringing someone else in, who may say they love me but have their own agenda or understanding of what love means. The biggest lesson was one of finding my own voice and my own power instead of continually seeking it in someone else. No one has our answers, no matter how hard or far we search. It's when we get lost within ourselves that we can appreciate putting down the map and exploring the edges of possibilities.

We're Living These Stories Over and Over

When we look at some of the biggest corporate scandals that have taken place on our planet, the mass media mostly report the financial losses associated with them. Rarely do they highlight what these scandals have meant for the lives of billions of people. One of the biggest collective financial scandals in history is the credit crisis of 2008, where Lehman Brothers and the Royal Bank of Scotland were deemed incompetent victims of events.

We may have a beautiful house or apartment, but working twelve hours a day keeps us from enjoying it. We may have a horrible boss who stresses us out to the point where it impacts our health, yet we still need to put food on the table for our family to survive. We may feel helplessly controlled by a system that forces us to sacrifice our health and well-being just to exist. Should we be deemed incompetent victims of events? Is there no other way?

This has to make us wonder if some people simply feel that the events unfolding on our televisions, computers, or mobile devices are occurring on a different plane of reality. It's as though we simply watch these events unfold in horror, and then discuss them in online forums or at dinner gatherings, but don't actually connect with them in any meaningful way or even recognize them as real. Yes, many of us feel the pain of a senseless shooting that takes human life, or a scandal, or a pandemic that keeps us locked up, or an economic scandal that wipes out individuals' life savings—but then we just seem to move on to the latest atrocity that is being reported in the media, and the fear only perpetuates, leaving us feeling outraged but helpless, until it knocks on our own door. It almost feels like we have somehow become used to disasters, moving from one to the next.

We can choose to remain as spectators and commentators of events, or we can take small or big actions that change this game to reflect our humanity in profound ways. Until we stop giving our power away and celebrating winners and losers in the public eye, the insanity will continue. What and who we consume matters more than we can ever imagine, as do the daily choices we make in what and who we invite into our lives. In the words of Machiavelli, known as the father of political philosophy, in *The Prince*, "The reason there will be no change is because the people who stand to lose from change have all the power. And the people who stand to gain from change have none of the power."

Isn't It Time to Write New Stories?

Here is a truth. It doesn't matter how stressful life gets, there is always a way forward. We may not like the choices in front of us, and it may be very difficult. But there is always a way. How we feel about taking risks says a lot about us. When it comes to risk, what matters is that we take the ones that matter most to us.

While there are some people who naturally take risks, there are others who stand back and wonder what they are missing by playing it safe. It all comes down to how we define success and failure. When our success is determined simply by comparing ourselves to everyone else, we'll always be a slave to other people's standards and needs. We learn to be safe, but safe can also be risky when we don't listen to our own heart.

The real question to ask is "Why can't I?" It's a question that always stays with us. We can choose to give up or to keep trying. Keep hoping that it will all work out and if not, there will be an important lesson in it. At the end of the day, what we are left with is knowing that we did our best and that we'll get up in the morning and try again. Are we ever truly ready? If we wait until we're ready we might be waiting forever. In the second installment of this series, we learn to trust ourselves so we can leap into the opportunity to trek into the unknown, and the third installment focuses on trusting our hearts as balanced creators.

Dealing with Our Resistance

In what way does the saying "If you always do what you've always done, you'll always get what you've always got" apply to you? Letting go means that it's up to us to change a pattern or break a mold. When an opportunity presents itself, how do you react? How do you respond to uncertainty or controversy? We probably can't rely on certainty anymore, so when we dare to be different, we can take a chance or decide to play with curiosity—the key is to be experimental and curious.

We are each wired with a certain level of resistance, and the challenge is identifying when it is healthy and helps us expand, and when it is unhealthy and restricts us. Resistance is simply a belief, a thought, a habit, or a behavior that constrains our energy. When resistance is present, we hold ourselves back and feel stuck because we're out of alignment. We could be stuck in a job or relationship that doesn't fulfill us, or it could be that we can't seem to find the exercise and diet that make us feel aligned with our body, no matter what we try. When we find ourselves feeling this way, we may be facing a voice telling us that it's too difficult to deal with the situation or person, or that there's nothing we can do to change it, or our irrational fear sets in. "This is how it has to be," we tell ourselves as we suffer through it. End of story.

But do you want to spend most of your waking hours living within those walls? There are steps you can take to get your resistance out of your way. Imagine you're hiking and you get to the end of the path where there are two huge mountains facing you. You drop to the ground and shake your head, wondering where these mountains came from, knowing there's no way you can climb them. It's way too strenuous for you and you can't do it—that's the track playing in your mind. You believe that you can only climb a mountain if you've given your body the attention it deserves, and you haven't.

You decide to camp at the foot of the mountain for the evening. You can start your trek up the mountain in the morning, after some rest, since going back is not an option. You spend the whole night awake, wondering how you got into this mess, feeling angry with yourself for not realizing the obstacles ahead of you. But you finally fall asleep and wake up to a hot ray of sun caressing your left cheek.

As you rub the sleep from your eyes, you sit up and can't believe what you're seeing, since you pitched your tent with your back to the mountains. You get up and right in front of you is a path that leads to roads and flowers running around the mountain. You feel your resistance subsiding as you enjoy the water from a nearby spring, as well as the apricots and figs generously offered by the abundant trees around you. As you continue to walk, you take this opportunity to take stock of the programs and beliefs running through you energetically and emotionally, and where they originated. Think about it like a garden—what seeds were planted, and what's growing in your garden? What weeds are trying to take over?

When you were lying on the ground feeling overwhelmed by having to climb the mountains ahead of you, and feeling as though you would never make it, you shifted your thoughts at one point to the idea that there had to be another way. When your belief that this potential exists is so strong, you're able to shift from a problem mindset to one of an opportunity creator. Maybe you even start to question everything, including whether you're resisting or standing in your own way. And perhaps you realize you were never told about the path of least resistance, which is always waiting for you to become aware of it.

The space between where we are in this moment and where we're heading requires us to be present and to align the thoughts and ideas flowing through us about what's possible. Changes taking place in our lives right now are necessary for healthy possibilities to arrive. Be at peace with these changes and carry a knowing within your heart that your current transition exists in preparation for a healthy life, where being aware of your resistance can free you.

When we focus on our energy, motivation, and *joie de vivre*, we align to our flow. We understand that a challenge or a struggle can be a trap of despondency for us to fall into when events don't go as planned. Any block of resistance can be seen as a reality check for us to realize that it might be healthier to extract our weeds and become aware of our limitations, moving in a direction that honors who we are. Consider the insight of author Howard Thurman, who wrote, "Don't ask yourself what the world needs. Ask yourself what makes you come alive, and go do that, because what the world needs is people who have come alive."

Comfort Is an Illusion Too

The notion that when we achieve success, we will not only be eternally happy but comfortable as well, is an illusion. Unless we're willing to sustain this feeling, it will only be fleeting when we finally get there! So, what then? A beneficial mindset and a skill to develop is learning how to be in the flow and constantly remain present.

The healthiest teacher is not always in the classroom, nor at the office, the workshop, the conference center, or on Zoom. The most amazing teacher we can have is around us every day: nature, and our own personal relationship with her. Nature is all-encompassing and requires our respect. If we live in a place that is susceptible to earthquakes or tornados, then it's wise to be prepared and adapt to living in that environment with emergency supplies and an evacuation plan in place. Rather than living in fear of an earthquake every day, we can continue to live our lives knowing we have a strategy and an infrastructure set up. As we have seen throughout 2020, life can change in a second, and panic and fear can spread like wildfire very quickly. Our comfortable lives can be disrupted in a flash by outside forces.

It's easy to lose pieces of ourselves in a sea of busyness. So how is it possible to feel disengaged when we are so connected and busy? We are taught that to be successful, it's necessary to be active 24/7 to fill our days and nights with activities. You may have been teased for staying in on a Friday or Saturday night, and made to feel unworthy if you are not busy doing something—but in March 2020, you may have found yourself in lockdown at home, and, depending on where you were in the world, you may have experienced a curfew or martial law a few months later. Because it may have stopped you from freely achieving your goals, you may have felt like a caged animal who was failing at life. But the real opportunity we had was to *slow down*.

Ask yourself, "How do I spend quality time with myself? When was the last time I simply enjoyed my own company and went with the flow of the moment?" I'm not talking about a vacation or a retreat. Sit and observe a body of water, like a lake or an ocean. Watch how it flows. Notice the ripples and current. Consider how the tiniest of movements carry the plankton or fish. It is simple, beautiful, and peaceful. There is no pursuit, there is no goal—only peace and harmony with our surroundings.

There is so much natural beauty in the world to learn from. One of the fallacies of modern living is that we must keep going, and we can forget to stop and take care of ourselves. It's time to remember that to be fully human, we have to take breaks and recharge. Nature has four seasons, and yet we somehow separate ourselves from the natural flow of the seasons. So many feel lonely but are unaware of the opportunity to enjoy the beauty and fierceness of our natural surroundings. We are never truly alone. Nature teaches us a great deal about letting go and flowing. The underground network of plants and fungi beneath our feet is always connected and intelligent. Mycologist Paul Stamets reminds us that "we need to have a paradigm shift in our consciousness. If we don't get our act together and come in commonality and understanding with the organisms that sustain us today, not only will we destroy those organisms, but we will destroy ourselves." One can only imagine that we will be able to be interconnected as below, so above.

Do you tend to cling to your familiar pain and forget you can rise above your tendency to stay small and hidden? Best-selling novelist Stephen King describes it aptly in his book *Joyland*: "It's hard to let go. Even when what you're holding onto is full of thorns, it's hard to let go. Maybe especially then."

Okay, take a deep breath. Breathe consciously and know that even in the darkest places of the mind, there is always a way forward. That breath is what keeps us alive and is one of the most important allies no one teaches us about. Thich Nhat Hanh, in the book *Stepping into Freedom*, shares this: "Feelings come and go like clouds in a windy sky. Conscious breathing is my anchor."

Growing Pains Are a Natural Part of the Journey

We're on a physical journey here, as we live and breathe every minute of every day. Do you take time to review and question your beliefs? Are you aware whose mental models you've adopted, and which ones are yours? Are you cognizant of which thoughts hold you hostage and what guidelines and rules are restraining you?

When we plant a seed in the earth, the seed will grow and develop into a plant. It's impossible to tell the seed to stay small and not grow. It's not feasible to convince the plant it is a seed and should not develop and blossom. We do, however, need to give it space to sprout and grow to reach its full potential. It needs to be nurtured and watered so it can thrive. Likewise, we need the same attention, otherwise we can get stuck in our principles or beliefs that limit our true potential.

What's possible has already happened and has been achieved, but the impossible is still here for us to discover and explore. What you see as impossible is unique to you. For someone who grew up in a remote village, a trip to a big city one hundred miles away may be viewed as a lifetime accomplishment. It all depends on our external environment and the values of the people we are surrounding ourselves with. We're stimulated and impacted by the world we live in. We are conditioned to strive, to constantly be in forward motion to achieve something. Therefore, depending on our circumstances, what is possible for one person may seem impossible to another.

The question is, what do you see as impossible? Is it something you find challenging and exciting enough to pursue with a healthy amount of vision and conviction?

We're Not Alone

Everyone on this planet is facing our own obstacles, shadows, or demons, and at the same time has opportunities that they may not yet recognize. Unfortunately, we don't regularly make time to sit down and understand the root cause of our problems or challenges. It's a bit insane that we can't see the abundant opportunities that surround us since we've been programmed to focus on the problems instead of the opportunities. Everything is a matter of what we want and how willing we are to work for it. As Albert Einstein said, "I am enough of the artist to draw freely upon my imagination. Imagination is more important than knowledge. Knowledge is limited. Imagination encircles the world."

Once you've decided where you're headed, and whether you're willing to get a bit lost along the way, you have to accept that pitfalls are inevitable and can't be avoided—but know that the journey will make you a stronger person. You'll have to be aware of potential rocks to climb and perhaps some steep crevices to overcome. You can prepare yourself at the outset to challenge yourself and perhaps even defeat the odds. Yes, you'll always have the option to quit and fall into the trap of blaming the world. No one can walk for you, but the most important thing is to believe in yourself enough to master your own journey.

It would be incredible to see more people intentionally come together to imagine and create together, to counteract the destruction, separation, and competition in a world striving for material achievement. One of the most powerful forces of our civilization is creativity. We have an opportunity to walk our talk and create meaningfully. Not just talk. We may think someone else has created the systems we find ourselves in, and yes, some humans did create them—but you can also choose to create the path for our time with systems that serve you and the collective. It could be a continuation with an improvement, a widening of the current systems, or the birthing of a healthier world.

What is happening on the edges is not the old world transforming itself, but a new world that is being born quietly. We're in the midst of this transition as we become more aware that this new, healthier world is emerging and we can play a role as a healthy creator of our life. It takes courage, as the road has not yet been paved.

It's the beginning of an unexpected and unpredictable adventure. It's not repeating what has been done before, with the mantras of innovation or disruption, but breaking away on our own exploration beyond that. It's a matter of healthy creation, with unforeseen events, risks, and opportunities. There are no maps to where we're going apart from tapping into our internal compass: our hearts, in alignment with our minds, bodies, and souls.

We already have everything we need, and the opportunity is to see it with the eyes of an architect, a healthy curiosity, and a commitment to learn from whatever shows up on this path.

Hitting the Pause Button

For some reason, many of us say we're too busy and don't have time to think. We simply focus on checking everything off our never-ending "to-do" lists to feel accomplished. We're in constant motion doing and achieving, which does not allow us time to pause and think.

But what happens when we put down the list and want to experience life instead of achieving success by knocking items off our lists? What if we choose to see a challenge that crosses our path as an opportunity to test ourselves? What if we knew it presented a chance to learn a new way to approach a problem and transform it into a success? What if we saw an opening to strengthen our ability to negotiate a situation and become a better communicator? Understanding the challenge is part of allowing ourselves to be able to let life flow. Those with an opportunity mindset can simply adjust and adapt to changes, and the changes become less dramatic and daunting.

Any complex situation can make us feel like we're stuck deep in the mud. When it comes to the reality of life, people get stuck in the mud all the time because we stop thinking and using our imagination to figure out how to get unstuck. Do you think that if you were desperate, stuck with no food or water, you would find a way to get some? What would you do to get yourself unstuck?

When you get addicted to comfort and safety, it actually paralyzes you. When you are paralyzed, you stop trusting your instincts and intuition. Staying connected to your intuition and one step ahead of your instincts will help you get out of tough situations. I always come back to this saying, often misattributed to German playwright and thinker Johann Wolfgang von Goethe: "Whatever you can do or dream you can—begin it. Boldness has genius, power, and magic in it." The key is to begin.

QUANTUM THINKING FOR OUR TIME

Our true reality is an ever-evolving, fluid experience, in which we're willing to face our own judgment and resolve within ourselves what has jailed our creative life force through constant sentencing. There are parts of us that have been stuck through experiences that have caused us pain at some point in our life. It could be that we were bullied at school or faced some other traumatic experience in life that keeps us in a cycle of shame, blame, intense embarrassment, or fear.

We may have had a narcissistic father or been abused as a child, or a war broke out in our country, or someone treated us poorly. There are so many things that happen to each of us that we have been taught to bury inside of ourselves. Becoming aware of where our pain comes from and where the voices in our heads originate is something no one teaches us. Instead, we're conditioned to smile and say we're okay, even when we're hurting deeply. But we don't have to carry this weight the rest of our lives, and we can get help to navigate and discover our wonder and joy.

When we become aware of the reason we suffer and start working on ourselves, we'll begin to see what has been lying dormant within us, waiting to create a healthy reality for us. Often something that happened ten or twenty years before remains with us as an unhappy or traumatic event. We don't need to carry it with us, but we can learn from it.

Memories have a way of pulling us back in time—and this happens mostly because when we remain attached to a certain event, we hold on to its negative energy. We don't just attach ourselves to the past, we're continuing to create the same situation in the present. There is beauty in learning to let go—which we will dive deep into in *F*ck the Bucket List for the Adventurer: Trekking into the Unknown,* in the Cleansing and Purging Expedition. There is absolutely no need to create this very same experience over and over, a process that defeats our entire well-being.

We can let go of past occurrences, even those that we've been deliberately holding on to because we remain angry and hurt about what happened. Attachment is something we may no longer want to replicate. When we attach our anger and fear to a specific event, we remain attached to its energy. We are creating an energetic frequency that is deeply rooted in that fear or limiting belief. As we're such powerful creators, we may find ourselves stuck, creating more of the same.

Once we become aware, we can shift our energy consciously. We can choose to release our attachment to survival and bring ourselves into the present moment. Once we do our deep inner work, we don't have to remain living the life of the victim—and perhaps we'll realize we never were a victim but simply made unhealthy choices for ourselves. There was regret, perhaps. Maybe the regret grew and grew until we just didn't know what to do with it. Then we hid the regret, along with its accompanying shame or other wounds, inside our being.

Resetting Our Hearts

If you're hurting right now and want to deal with your hurt, do your research and find a professional who can help you, or start having deep conversations with yourself. If you do want external help, love yourself by doing impeccable research to find someone who resonates with you and understands what you're going through. If you are a veteran, find someone who understands where you've been and where you want to go. There are people wanting to help, but it's not always simple to find each other within the constructs of our broken systems.

Many people are going through difficult times, but it's not socially acceptable (yet) to openly discuss the increasing need we have to deal with all the trauma that's bouncing around our planet. It's much easier to condition ourselves to be heroes who mask our pain. That cannot be our way forward, as our lives matter deeply and we have an opportunity to support ourselves and each other. We've been gifted with more than we can ever imagine and we can change the programming of the stories we've been fed.

Be in your power to decide whether the person is healthy or unhealthy for you by trusting your intuition and feeling deeply into your body for how they resonate with your energy—and if you feel that they don't get you, don't suck it up or suffer. This is your life and you get to navigate according to your own compass.

People can help, but no one has your answer. Boundaries that are broken help us clear the way for fresh experiences that are more aligned with what we want to explore on our life's journey. Every breath allows us to go deep inside and get aligned with what is waiting to be unleashed. Self-awareness is the path to changing a belief, so as we fully understand what has taken place, even the most stubborn neural pathways of the past start to rewire themselves effortlessly.

Ask yourself, "What is the first step I can take right now in this moment? What is within my control?"

EXPEDITION 6

THERE'S ALWAYS A WAY

We're living in transformational times. What too often seems impossible can become possible when we step out of the overwhelming noise and fear of the modern world. There are no lists, manuals, or road maps to where we're headed, as we're the ones creating them. We've already been given abundant tools—such as imagination, curiosity, courage, sadness, and hope—and the rest is up to us to imagine, create, and produce.

Our world continues to go through dramatic change, improbable advancements, and game-changing breakthroughs. Public personalities will continue to be hailed or criticized. Internal and external wars and competitions will be won and lost. Blame and outrage will continue to dominate the reactions to the injustices of this world. And, at the same time, there will be a growing realization that people like you and me can transform our lives when we start seeing the invisible barriers that are holding us hostage through fear, anger, judgment, blame, division, cynicism, or loneliness.

In her book *When Things Fall Apart,* author Pema Chödrön provides advice for challenging times: "To be fully alive, fully human, and completely awake is to be continually thrown out of the nest. To live fully is to be always in no-man's-land, to experience each moment as completely new and fresh. To live is to be willing to die over and over again."

RELEASING OURSELVES FROM THE PRISON OF THE MIND

Many of us are now starting to realize that we've been living inside a box with invisible prison walls that have been constructed through years of societal conditioning of how life should be, or self-inflicted by our own belief systems and stories. More and more people are silently experiencing an increasing desire to break free from this box and the fear it keeps us chained to.

For many, it's hard to admit how imprisoned we are by fear. Fear of being judged by others, of not having enough, or of not being good enough. Yet those we fear, who criticize us, are also often incarcerated by their own fears and shadows. It takes courage and curiosity to break free from the walls manufactured by society and discover who we truly are outside these structures. Our mind collects and stores memories, containing a virtual file cabinet filled with our deepest disappointments and failures. Many of us find ourselves deeply attached to these disappointments.

The impressions of everyone and everything that has ever disappointed us is not only locked within us, but also keeps spinning inside us. We have been conditioned to base our lives and futures on our stories of disappointment and our deep failures. I learned in a voice and speech class I took as part of my early theatre training that many of these emotions and traumas are locked inside our physical body. A practitioner who understands trauma can unlock some of our most painful experiences by finding the spot in our back where we have locked our emotional pain away. I had this happen when I was in a session and not only experienced the physical pain but also the deep release of memories. It was surreal when I heard the practitioner tell me how she saw me as a young child experiencing war. At the time, I rarely talked about it publicly and kept it hidden inside of me.

Some of us are not aware that we carry these burdens in our shoulders, necks, and backs everywhere we go. We can only release them by doing inner work and deep body work like massage—starting by becoming aware of the deeply rooted programming we're carrying inside and choosing to release it. Flour doesn't become bread without yeast helping it rise and forming through a little heat.

Notice how your body reacts. Do you relax and immediately feel at ease to engage in conversation, or do you become guarded and reserved? Your intuition will signal to you that you are in a healthy place or it will feel artificial and you will know it. You're hardwired and have the ability to listen to your own intuition.

The time is now to pause and reflect on the opportunities that are right in front of you. Every time you interact with another person—be it a stranger, a grocery store clerk, or someone you pass on the street—it is a chance to learn to speak with a fellow human being and navigate your path to the best of your ability.

Consider how you connect with people around you and throughout your day. Do you make assumptions and miss opportunities to interact and get to know people, and are you remembering to take the time to build bridges?

What if Failure and Disappointment Are Opportunities to Grow?

Every day, instead of thinking about your failures and disappointments, you can think about what you learned and how you evolved. If you're reading this, then you most definitely woke up this morning, while many did not. You may have taken a walk and moved your body. You may have read a story to a child who laughed uncontrollably with pure joy. You may have listened to someone having a challenging day, or it may have been you who was having a lousy day. You may have smiled at a stranger who smiled back at you—at a distance, from behind their mask.

We "succeed" on many levels throughout our day, but we don't always see these successes as important. We reference the places we've failed or the times we were disappointed more often in our minds. We criticize and judge ourselves for saying the wrong thing or wearing the wrong outfit. Our future is based on a labyrinth of failures and disappointments.

Many of us have learned to sabotage ourselves. It's this continual sabotaging that keeps us feeling "less than" and running in circles of stress and burnout. Our suitcases are filled with a never-ending need to prove ourselves, to feed our next high in an imbalanced world of expectations and winning at all costs.

All we can do is become increasingly self-aware of our actions and reactions. When we make peace within ourselves, when we address our hurt, then we can start letting go of the pain of our deepest disappointments. There are no real wars to fight when we focus on our inner peace. Then, and only then, have we done our part to shift from seeing everything as a problem to coming together to address our opportunities.

What if each societal failure was an opportunity to shift the future into a place we desired to be? What if every day we reminded ourselves and others of our breakthroughs and growth instead of our failures? We could re-pattern our minds and hearts, opening a doorway within ourselves to higher levels of creation.

What Happens When Internal Recognition Is More Important than Applause?

William Shakespeare wrote, "All the world's a stage . . . and one man in his time plays many parts." The type of stories playing out on our individual stage depends on how we engage with ourselves and the people in our lives. When we have unhealthy people performing, we often find ourselves in tragedies, dramas, or even horror shows. Our energy gets swept away by the story until the next performance.

We can birth ourselves anew each day, but no one applauds our efforts, our insights, our dedication, and our breakthroughs. Where is the applause and recognition when we believe we need them most? Where is the validation our ego seeks? How will we attain our next high and declare success? A great depression has afflicted the human race, an all-encompassing hopelessness, a sense of giving in and giving up. A fight for our very lives plays out with all that happens to divide us and continue the energy of hurt and outrage. And yet, look at what powerful creators we all are.

People in the spiritual community instruct us that there are two people on stage: one as our ego-driven, physical body and the other as our true, spiritual self. We spend part of our life in conflict to let our soul guide us and connect with who we really are spiritually. The people who show up in our lives are there to love and support us, teach us, or cause us great disturbance. No matter what, we can all show up to play a role in helping with the growth of our soul.

It doesn't really matter what story we believe, but what we do know is that throughout most of our lifetime we've been expected to wear different masks—including the mask that disguises our true feelings. We put another coat of paint on the house to mask the fact that the foundation is rotting. We put on our happy face even when the sadness in our heart seeps through our bones. We've been expected to perform on stage, and usually it is we who give ourselves invisible ratings on how we did, depending on the level of applause or validation we received during each performance.

Our nightly review, before we go to sleep, is an opportunity to look back at our day and think about what transpired. We get a chance to think about our day and review how it unfolded—but what if we did it with a healthy perspective? What if we recognized a lesson that we're grateful for instead of punishing ourselves for what we've been taught to believe as being stupid? It helps to think about something that touched us and let the positive energy flood into us—and when someone or something keeps haunting us, we can ask ourselves, why are we giving it energy? Why is it taking up space in our mind? And does it need to continue occupying space?

When we start focusing on who and what is healthy in our lives, we can give ourselves a break. We can understand what's going on inside of ourselves and acknowledge our balance or imbalance. John Lennon reminds us that "when you do something noble and beautiful and nobody noticed, do not be sad. For the sun every morning is a beautiful spectacle and yet most of the audience still sleeps." It's up to us to recognize that we don't need to keep performing for the applause. We can also move into our hearts by becoming aware that everyone around us is going through something.

FINDING OUR WAY IN A WORLD OF LABELS

Imagine a world where we can see and know each other for who we truly are without any labels to define our wealth, our culture, our ethnicity, our marital status, or our sexual orientation. We know this is an enormous undertaking, but it is worth seeking in the vastness of life.

Every time we watch the news, we are consuming someone else's opinions and agendas. We are seeing the world and its problems through another perspective. The challenge to stay abreast of what is going on in the world is to find healthy ways to obtain information. The most reliable source is to connect firsthand with the people involved. We now have the technology to do that. The real question is, do we know how to connect with healthy people to get to what we're creating?

It's pretty simple. Anyone who has access to electricity and a computer can connect to the internet. How we consume and digest information is different for each one of us. Building community and connecting with others is possible by finding our own way to connect with anyone in the world. It often just takes a lot of hard work to find each other.

Technology, like humans, is not evil at its core. It all depends on whether we choose to use it in a healthy or toxic way. One story is that the internet was born out of the imagination of computer scientists Vinton Cerf, Bob Kahn, and Tim Berners-Lee, who together imagined the World Wide Web. Its ultimate goal was to fulfill curiosity and connect people, making knowledge available to all. It is an opportunity to create our own menu or to feed on our prescribed lunch box—it's our choice.

We Have More at Our Fingertips Than We Could Ever Imagine

Everything could be at our disposal should we explore healthy paths and create what is missing and needed. Compassion and understanding starts with us. Taking off the limiting labels, which give us a tag, and stepping into a true depiction of who we are, is a genuine opportunity to take the first step that's calling us.

Labels can strangle us, or they can give us comfort. People pride themselves on being sports fans and even wear the team colors to identify themselves. It gives them a sense of belonging and a community to connect with when they gather at the lounge bar or get coffee in the morning at the café. The group comradery is infectious as they talk about the game, wins and losses. However, when we're not part of the group or don't own the right uniform, we're left standing alone and feeling excluded.

We're constantly divided into groups. It's essential to be conscious of this and to be aware of the labels and see if they still work for us. This is not about rejecting our favorite team but questioning whether we're part of the group because we truly love it and its purpose, or because of the status symbol it brings or a desire to belong.

So much of our society has grown into artificial connections, which creates assumptions that because someone belongs to a certain group, they share the same values and perspectives and get lumped into the same judgments. We forget to take the time to truly build trusted relationships, because we are too busy running like a hamster on a wheel, rushing from one activity to another, to build our social status.

There are organic communities emerging out of a need for a purpose or passion to contribute to humanity's growth. Every day brings a learning opportunity, and it is good to approach it with curiosity. Of course, we naturally gravitate to similar faith-based beliefs and geographic locations, but what excites us and gets the heart pounding is when there is a pure connection with like-minded souls. There are many opportunities to connect with people in the same affiliated community, or somewhere unexpected, if you are willing to imagine what your intentional community looks like.

What's the Opportunity to Truly Connect?

Ancient civilizations migrated because they were curious to search what was beyond the hill. They tapped into their imagination and dreamed about what they'd discover when they kept moving along unexplored paths. Today, we have Google Earth to travel and explore on the internet, allowing us to view stunning landscapes and gorgeous places around the globe. All we have to do is type a location or address in the search bar, and we'll be taken right to the street name. We can even zoom in or out to see the topography up close or from a greater perspective via satellites. We can go to practically any place in the world and learn how people live and observe their environment.

Technology is transforming communities and future neighborhoods. Instead of going out to the local shops for food and goods, people are ordering products online through our devices. This is very much a solo action, a one-way conversation without any interaction with a live person. This small change affects a community and even human behavior.

The art of interaction with each other is being lost. Indeed, the smallest interaction with a sales assistant provides a connection with another human being and in essence feeds the spirit and soul of a city. Humans need to connect with one another. It's a fundamental, core issue for a healthy person to thrive. Limiting the amount of exposure to other individuals and one-on-one contact is creating a crisis in the world. We witness all too often in the news the tragic mass shootings by lonely individuals who feel disrespected and unheard. Too much focus is placed on the technology or platforms to voice opinions, and not enough on integrating the value of the content into benefiting life. In ancient communities, people gathered, had conversations and made decisions on a daily basis. Maybe human connection and dialogue are ancient technologies that many of us are missing in our daily life today?

Who Created Loneliness?

What is loneliness? The Oxford Dictionary defines it as "solitary, without companionship, and isolated." An article in *Psychology Today* in 2014 addressed its impact on the psyche by going deeper and stating, "Loneliness does not depend on how many friends or relationships you have but whether you feel emotionally and/or socially disconnected from those around you." Feeling lonely distorts our perception of relationships, devaluing them and making us withdraw even further. The article stipulated that loneliness is contagious in social networks, and attracts and compounds the misery of seclusion and exclusion.

We now have an epidemic in the Western world of lonely people. While it's reported with facts and figures, the root cause is not being explored or addressed. Burnout and loneliness are seen as mental health issues that require medication. Our current use of technology is part of this problem, allowing individuals to be self-sufficient by ordering online and socializing through social media platforms. These websites invite and encourage us to share the highs and lows of our life in great detail, on a stage with pictures and video, but without any real person-to-person connection. Many users tend to compare their lives with those of others, and unless we're part of the celebration or the tragedy, we feel left out and begin to withdraw, causing great loneliness.

One of the biggest travesties we have today is that it's super challenging to find each other and connect, based on what we want to create in the world, from healthy education, to financial, to health care systems. And most of the connections are still by word-of-mouth despite the plethora of online platforms. The irony is that we're brilliant beings and yet we let the material world control us. Humans have created tools to find a ride (ridesharing apps), places to stay (accommodation apps), a hookup for the night (hookup apps for every sexual orientation), and networks (social apps to post selfies, market, and advertise), and so many more "inventions" show up in apps every day.

But at the same time, some are starting to create amazing mental health, meditation, and mindfulness apps, like Get A-Head®, created by a team of mental health experts to combat some of the barriers people face in getting care, which include anonymity, accessibility, and relatability. It is the brainchild of a remarkably visionary man, Ahad Bandealy, who suffered from depression and felt a need to create something he wished he'd had, and which can help billions of people on our planet.

Artistology® is a collaborative community for creatives—Where Artists Thrive.™ As a music industry pioneer, Tammy McCrary founded Artistology® because she believes that "artists are the cultural architects of society. There is a direct correlation between the messages that are delivered through music, film, television and gaming and the society that is manifested. I believe that when artists thrive – mentally, emotionally, spiritually, physically and financially – they can have a significant and positive impact on society. When the artist thrives, humanity survives!" Her mission is to provide a safe and trusted community offering wellness resources for artists where they can connect and collaborate with other artists who get them and obtain resources that empower them. It's no coincidence that Get A-Head® and Artistology® are now collaborating and co-creating what's needed most in the world.

We can connect when we set the intention and do a ton of work; it takes a great deal of effort and energy. Right now, at this moment, I believe that maybe 2 percent of the 7.7 billion people on this planet may be ready for the F*ck the Bucket List series. While that's a lot of people, connecting remains challenging as this is not a self-help, spiritual, or memoir book or a mainstream hashtag. If I wanted to find and engage with the people ready for these specific books, there is yet to be a place to find each other, especially to connect in dialogue, after experiencing the books. There is no app for the pioneers and architects of humanity where we could have open conversations about what matters most to us. Most of the introductions still happen through people we know. And most of the platforms have only touched the surface when it comes to creating the online communities we truly need, where everyone has a voice and dialogue is powered by the technology, not the other way around.

It's an illusion that we can easily find each other on the internet, and while there is some ease, we're not taking care to connect with the people physically around us. There are hundreds of thousands of chat groups online. We can reach out to people from all over the world when we have a device and internet connectivity. The belief is that if we have a device, we're not alone. And yet, so many people are feeling alone and lonely. Many of the platforms divide us even further with online debates that can often turn ugly, with people easily hiding behind their screens or pseudonyms.

The Buddha said, "What you dwell upon you become." The more people feed the issue, the more it deepens, widens, and eventually starts crossing oceans so that the ripple effect casts further afield to include more people in a sea of isolation. And yet this is a great opportunity; instead of reporting statistics and discussing problems, it is an opportunity to discover solutions and dig a path out of our collective mess. It's an opportunity to resurrect, in spirit, and innovate on foundational platforms like The Well, or CompuServe in the late 1980s, that bring people together in dialogue.

A great deal of our collective loneliness comes from the fact that we've been taught that happiness comes from outside ourselves, and that is simply untrue. Sure, eating our favorite dessert or seeing our favorite musician can bring us much joy, but it's not sustainable beyond the transaction and the time we're engaged in the activity.

True happiness comes from being happy with yourself. Yes, this is true. Notice the people around you, and you'll see that healthy and whole people are happy within ourselves—with being able to be who we are at the core. When was the last time you asked yourself, "What makes me happy?" or "When do I experience pure joy?" Did you take the time to listen to yourself answer this question, or did you rush off and take care of someone else's needs first?

A Little Less Blaming Allows Us to Open Windows of Self-Awareness

Yes, we can blame technology for the increased isolation in our society, but technology alone isn't at fault. When we look back on our history, we'll notice different periods—such as the Middle Ages, the Renaissance, and the Industrial Age—and see that each era had its own revolution and growing pains. The invention of the lightbulb in the twentieth century brought one of the biggest disruptions humanity has ever experienced, and yet very few blame the lightbulb for the chaos it caused in our lives. This one invention allowed us to increase productivity and efficiency in the workplace, as people could now work around the clock, and the night shift was born.

Today, the smartphone has replaced the lightbulb, making it possible to connect with other people 24/7 and challenging the forty-hour, five-day workweek business model. The lightbulb effect has morphed into mobile devices, changing our relationships in both business and personal arenas, and disrupting the way we used to balance how we spent our time. And today, we live in a world where everything is vying for our attention. So many of us are too stressed out to take a breath and see what's truly going on.

We can stay conscious of our immediate surroundings as opportunities to connect. By handing over our power to our devices, we're allowing *them* to sit in the driver's seat and drive us. Perhaps we may feel less lonely when we put our focus on what is right in front of us and engage with it—be it cooking, baking, nature, films, reading, playing, etc. This will allow us to integrate and use the technologies that we find valuable to enhance our life instead of seeing them as another place to go.

There Is No Destination—We're Here to Experience Everything

We've all been told the story that happiness is a destination, and we need to get there in order to experience it. But where is *there*? *There* is here, now—the present moment when you're reading or listening to this book. The best way to understand the meaning of being happy in the present moment is personal. We can learn a lot by spending time in nature, or being with animals, for example. Nature and animals live in the now. They cannot exist anywhere else but in the present. They live totally in harmony with universal law. We can't tell a rose bush or a tree not to grow. The bush and tree are completely content being and living in the environment, and they adjust to the weather conditions and seasons to develop.

Take a walk in the woods or a stroll on a beach on a stormy day, and feel the connection to nature and her immense power. People who live in residential developments, which have imposed on the natural habitats of the wildlife, often play a territorial game with their animal neighbors. The deer that wander into the garden and start eating flowers and vegetables are confused when they are told it's off limits. We build a fence to reinforce the rules, to keep the animals out, but they don't understand.

Illusions such as division or ownership don't exist in nature; everything is fair game, and everyone is free to roam wherever they'd like. A dog may rip up the couch when left alone at home as he experiences separation anxiety. But would he do the same if he was outside the home and not someone's pet? Loneliness happens to any being separated from the intelligence of nature. We can choose to buy into our deep divide or decide how to understand it, so we can deconstruct it and take down the walls and feelings of separation and isolation.

What, If Anything, Is Boxing Us In?

Loneliness and depression around the world are, sadly, at an all-time high. In 2017, the UK government appointed a Minister of Loneliness, as more than nine million people in the country admitted to feeling lonely, according to a report published by the Jo Cox Commission on Loneliness. The study found that loneliness is worse for your health than smoking fifteen cigarettes a day. It was determined that loneliness is among the greatest cause of cardiovascular disease, dementia, depression, and anxiety. Dr. Vivek Murthy, a former United States surgeon general, wrote an article for the *Harvard Business Review* advocating that loneliness be addressed in the workplace.

How do we become lonely and isolated? By cutting ourselves off from ourselves, family, or friends; by being unable to honestly express our emotions, and feeling as though we're not being heard; and by failing to coexist regularly with nature. If we believe we're not part of the team at work—if it feels unsafe or unwelcome to express our opinions or contribute to the groups we're part of in our department—the natural human response is to withdraw. This often leads to feelings of being unrecognized or unacknowledged, and also leads to feeling unable to celebrate our successes with our colleagues. We retreat from society as we feel invisible and overlooked. These compounded feelings build and perpetuate, as we believe we are the only ones feeling this way. Maybe living in a box contributes to these feelings?

Feeling alone is the first place to start, believe it or not. Acknowledging where we are at the moment is the first power point at which to begin. Every feeling comes from a story. A story in this scenario is an incident or episode in our life that made a huge impression on us. Healing ourselves from a personal story that impacted us negatively can be extremely difficult and sometimes very painful.

We are creatures of habit. If we're willing to look back, we'll see a pattern emerge, whether it's romantic partners, friends, organizations we gravitate to, communities we live in, workplaces, or conflicts we attract. We may see the same person appearing as a character in our life with a new name or head. Until we learn that they are here to teach us, a new person with the same lesson will appear, and only when we can break the pattern can we let go of the need to attract this character into our life.

To take responsibility for your well-being, you can start by identifying the box you are in and naming the walls that keep you imprisoned within it. Go back in time and look for the root of your pain—the original wound—and see how it is repeating itself in the present moment.

This is the path to "staging an intervention" and preventing the pattern from repeating again and again. You must revisit and confront one of the most difficult times in your life and challenge yourself to look at the incident objectively. Being able to look honestly at our problems and see the opportunities within them allows us to have a greater understanding of the lessons we need to learn.

There Are No Quick Fixes on the Road to Being Human

We've collectively created or inherited a fast-food culture where we expect instantaneous results and quick fixes for whatever ails us. But what if we took a minute to ask ourselves what our lives are all about? Do we rush from one snack to the next, not fully experiencing each one or feeling satisfied—or do we want to truly experience life to the fullest? Are we aware of our opportunity to put down the manual of success, which we were given by a parent, teacher, or spiritual guide, and discover our own path by seeing the choices we're making and what is possible for us on this journey?

Society teaches us, for example, that being angry is not acceptable. And yet, being angry is a fundamental emotion along with sadness, happiness, and love. It's absolutely okay to feel angry—how we *express* anger, however, is important to monitor. It's very healthy to understand our anger, and it's crucial to become aware of what triggers it. Suppressing it and storing it inside us is unhealthy. Much like a pressure cooker, it can explode at any moment.

Being sad is part of being human—like being happy—but we don't have to live in our house (box) of sadness forever. We can become aware of why we feel this way by going back to the original wound and becoming aware that we don't have to live in a world of hurt. We can also control the amount of hurt we're being exposed to by understanding that we didn't come to this planet to suffer.

FULLY EXPERIENCING LIFE IS THE CORNERSTONE OF THIS ADVENTURE

Not everyone is guided by a pure, beautiful purpose. There are people in the world who are on a journey of destruction with hearts filled with hatred and fear. They are stuck in this mindset, and we need to be aware of how their intentions can impact our lives. There are also many nonprofit organizations with professed noble purposes which express the attitude that because, for example, they are reducing poverty, they can treat their employees poorly. The deeper underlying question here is "Are you doing harm to yourself and/or others? And if so, why is this the course you're on?"

We each come to life with our own beliefs and outlooks. Anyone experiencing the current state of the environment—politics, economy, and society—can see parts of it as being either inspirational or traumatic. We can take a walk in a forest or attend a Rolling Stones concert and feel inspired, or we can be deeply traumatized by the plastic and garbage floating in the ocean, or the impending honeybee colony collapse, which will ultimately impact our access to food. All of these experiences are real and surround us.

As with the end of feudalism 500 years ago, people have the power to create and birth something new. Increasing access to information through technology is helping to create a new route that can be healthy or destructive, depending on how we consume information. When we realize that our decisions matter, that we and others can create something more dynamic and inclusive than what exists, we'll look at the current systems and ask different questions. We don't need to start outside of ourselves; we can become aware of where and how we can reshape our lives to be the best we can be without competing or taking anyone else down.

A friend posted her opinion online of how a *real* man should behave. People are holding on so tightly to their definitions of how others should behave. There are all these beliefs and standards that we are expected to live up to when we buy into the existing story. It can be exhausting. But we can also become aware that there's another way, and the choice is not between idolizing a real man and pointing fingers at one we shame for not living up to our standards. The irony is that the man my friend chose to highlight as a real man is someone I have researched and found to be deeply corrupt. But that's not the point; the point is that we continue to fight and take sides over who's right on this, or on any belief system. It doesn't hurt me for her to hold on to her beliefs.

Imagine a world where our purpose is aligned with our higher goals channeled to us through our intuition. Our opportunities become more expansive, bright, and beautiful when we let go of limiting beliefs. When we spend as much time and effort caring about the well-being of people at work as we do the security of our systems and data, we'll experience healthier outcomes. This era is about breaking free from our own unnecessary constraints and waking up to what is possible.

There's no longer a need to live within someone else's paradigm. What happens when we face our biggest limiting beliefs head-on so that we can do the work we're meant to? Change is happening every day, despite what the mainstream media may want us to believe, and some people are reimagining their lives one step at a time. There is no need to rush. Nature doesn't rush.

We Are at an Intersection

There are viruses of the mind—fed to humanity, equally, through fear. And yet, we don't have to allow unhealthy fear to restrict our lives in any way. We become healthy when we keep our minds virus-free and ground ourselves in possibilities, leaving irrational fear at the curb. This is no small feat and rather an opportunity for those of us ready to create a healthy life. Just like washing our hands, we can cleanse our minds and reduce our susceptibility to infection.

This is a time when many of us are being tested on how entrenched we are in the traditional system. We are being asked to examine whether we can break free from viruses that have been infecting our minds for decades. There are people who don't want the entrenched system to change and serve the vast majority of humanity. They are hanging on for dear life, hoping that we continue to consume what they have to offer, thereby allowing the system to continue to support their interests. We have created a celebrity culture where a few get elevated and rewarded for being the best and having the most. The more we feed their entrenched interests, the more imprisoned we are in their beliefs of how the world should be.

We're at an intersection. We can buy into the fear and strengthen its message by consuming it, or we can choose not to allow fear to restrict our lives. This is a test of our mental and physical immune systems. We can live our lives and recognize irrational fear for what it is. Of course, we don't want to walk into oncoming traffic or cuddle a black bear—those are rational instincts to have—but we can each start assessing what we're being fed and what we choose to consume in our daily diet.

Often we find ourselves struggling, facing a transition or a trauma, and when someone stops and asks us how we're doing, we either involve them in every detail of our story or say nothing and smile. It's so challenging when we're deep into whatever is unfolding in our lives—such as our kids being unreasonable, hearing about another loss or illness, or simply having a crappy day. It all enters our reality.

There's a tool available to us. Think of a scale where on one side sits the unhealthy and stress-inducing activities in your life, and on the other side are the healthy ones. Are you in balance or out of balance? In the midst of it all, you can examine your scale, and if you have access to taking a breath, assess what it is that you need. Is it information, support, healing, awareness, clarity, or a reasonable person to talk to? How can you pause and become an observer of your situation through a different perspective?

When we feel someone or something dragging us down, can we ask ourselves why we're giving them our attention and energy? Can we identify a pattern that creates imbalance for us and causes us suffering?

When we live in the present, we have less need to rush, which in turn creates more harmony and less stress. When we live in the present, we're no longer focused on what's next or an ultimate destination. This, in turn, gives strength to our minds and bodies. When we feel out of balance and need to rest, or when we face ailments or poor health, we might need to step back from the insanity of modern life and cultivate a more present and peaceful state of mind. How can we cultivate balance by listening to our inner voices and being fully present?

We can become aware of the stories in our minds and understand whether they have been planted there, after years of conditioning, or whether they're ours. We don't have to stay entrenched. Finding inner peace and balance allows us to expand into our wonder. Balance is love, and love doesn't judge.

Coming Face-to-Face with Spirituality as a Business

There is abundant wisdom and advice from ancient times to today about learning about the world and how we react to life. Plato shared, "Reality is created by the mind. We can change our reality by changing our mind." Jesus said, "It is done unto you as you believe." Hindu mysticism tells us that "whatever a person's mind dwells on intensely and with firm resolve, that is exactly what he becomes." The Talmud observes, "We do not see things as *they* are, we see them as *we* are." Ralph Waldo Emerson wrote, "We become what we think about all day long." Napoleon Hill said, "Whatever the mind can conceive and believe it can achieve."

At one point in my journey, I learned that despite what I've been taught, I was not only personally responsible for my health and well-being, but also for my experiences. The more I started to see reality for what it was, the more questions I had, and it was not easy finding people who wanted to talk openly about what we were truly experiencing beyond the smoke and mirrors.

When I started digging deep, I found a whole bunch of New Age stuff, theories and gurus, all vying for my attention. There were so many workshops, readings, and retreats I had never been aware of being offered in every part of the world. It was so confusing to see an entirely different world and realize that there was a version of spirituality that was also a big business. There were businesses popping up everywhere that claimed to have my answer, spewing Rumi, Carl Jung, and Alan Watts. They told me that we were just a reflection of everyone who shows up in our lives and that we *create our own reality* without considering the physical reality around us. There is still a very real physical reality we exist in where we might cross a road and get run over by a bus—like my grandmother did. There is also a metaphysical reality that scientists like Albert Einstein and Max Planck shined a light on. We can seek enlightenment everywhere we go, but what many of us struggle with is integrating the worlds and finding a way not to go to battle every day.

Regardless of what was happening around me, I realized that what mattered was how I responded and perceived the experiences in my life. I learned that even when life becomes challenging, my mindset matters in how I react to the physical reality, while I sharpen my ability to listen to my intuition more and more about what is real and what I can create in my life. When I could see opportunities, instead of problems, everywhere I went, I started to experience life in a healthier way. These were all lessons learned as I met more and more gurus who were there to hold my hands and wallet while I went through the *dark night of the soul*—a stage where we undergo a significant transition to a deeper perception of life and our place in it, which often forces us to shed our identity, relationship, career, habits, or belief systems.

Some of these gurus claimed to be great manifesters, attracting whatever they wished for into their reality, and I agreed, since they were getting monetarily wealthy from those who followed them. I've been studying cults and deprogramming since I was thirteen years old, and I could see that our world was a sort of cult that teaches us to follow blindly. There were new gurus appearing all over the planet in white robes, adorned in gems and sometimes long beards, all wanting to be our spiritual guides.

I also discovered a wealth of information on aliens, the hyper-dimensional matrix, and colonizing Mars. We can just search for it online if we want to experience it. On Facebook I came across the great-granddaughter of US President Dwight David Eisenhower, Laura Eisenhower, who reveals information about his administration that has been largely held in secrecy. She also writes and speaks openly about hidden agendas and putting a stop to human trafficking of children. I was fascinated by how many different theories were out there—but I also learned to trust my own intuition as to what resonated and what didn't, with an openness and curiosity to simply learn about aspects of our world I never knew were out there.

IT'S UP TO US TO STOP THE INSANITY

For me, it was overwhelming to see how noisy this New Age world was. So I decided to stop searching and start listening to my inner guidance to trust whatever information, data, or person I resonated with. It took practice to weed out what resonated with me from what I felt was unhealthy for me. I met some delusional people on my path, who were not a reflection of me but were great teachers of how I did *not* want to live my life. I realized I was here to experience the circle of life and not be someone else's consumer or follower. Nature was my guide to understanding that the deep-rooted connections below my feet—consisting of plants and fungi working in community—could also happen aboveground with a healthy focus.

Many of the systems I was taught to trust implicitly were starting to crack. When I spoke to teachers and educators, they shared that while their roles were to prepare the next generation, they didn't really know what jobs they were preparing the next generation for. To add to that, there was no ongoing dialogue with the very people who, in essence, will be our future workforce, about what jobs might be needed for the future. We have an amazing opportunity to sit down with young people and, together, imagine and co-create what their future might look like. And we even have an opportunity to help teachers be role models for questioning, dialogue, and co-creation, should we choose to step out and explore possibilities.

It's becoming increasingly apparent that in the future (and even now), jobs may not provide or fulfill. Today and in the future, governments may not have our best interests at heart. The celebrated success metrics that once made us proud may start feeling empty and meaningless. What will most likely dawn on us is that living within these constructs may not seem as easy anymore, and safety as we know it is not guaranteed.

The younger generation has witnessed the overconsumption habits of Western culture among their parents' and grandparents' generations. They feel stuck and overburdened. As life expectancy has increased dramatically, young people now also carry the responsibility of taking care of two generations. When I gave a talk at the South by Southwest conference in Austin, Texas, a young woman contributed greatly to the conversation by reminding us that while she carried a huge student debt, she is now "responsible for not just taking care of my parents but also their parents because life expectancy has increased."

The cracks in the seemingly solid constructs that we've built to guide and protect ourselves are starting to show—and when we step away from the mainstream and New Age chatter, we can experience the questioning that is taking place. We may feel helpless and hopeless, which is truly understandable, as we start peeling back the layers of reality. We might think there is nothing we can do at the beginning, but over time, these and other questions may pop up for you: What can I do? What else is possible? Why am I here? How do I address my pain? What does joy mean to me? What do I want to create?

It's easy to throw in the towel and dream of walking away from all our responsibilities. But our rent or mortgages still need to be paid, and we need a source of income to cover them. We can pick up and run away to a cave or yurt in a forest, but if we do that, we'll simply shut ourselves off from the world and not necessarily deal with what is in front of us—which is patiently asking us to face it on a much deeper level.

Feeling into Life Itself

When you feel that everything in your life and the world around you is out of control, pay attention to how you define control. What needs to be controlled? In a world where life and death are symbiotic, should we not let some things unravel and die so healthier things can emerge? Some people look at me funny when I tell them that I feel like I am in between two worlds: the one that is here and is becoming increasingly unhealthy as a way of life for me and the vast majority of people, and the one that is emerging from people who are discovering and creating healthier lives. There are so many amazing things happening in our world that rarely make it to the news. But when we have access to holistic news platforms that people are quietly building in back rooms, our field of vision will expand, as will our curiosity for creation.

So much of what I held dear and believed to be true, and what made me feel safe, is dead or dying or on life support. But instead of feeling like a victim of circumstance, I'm living with renewed awareness and a deep desire to find the other architects of humanity who are constructing healthy lives and systems ranging from education to business. Sure, it has been heartbreaking to see that the constructs and signposts that have been my guides are not trustworthy. I can more clearly see that people simply agreed to ways we should live and made us believe it was the only way, and to focus merely on progress and innovation as metrics of evolution, and protest and outrage as ways of participation.

But in reality, these systems are hurting many of the people on earth. In a world of abundance of opportunity, we can create healthy systems rather than suffer through life, or even try to create a "better" or "improved" world. "Better" continues to divide us in judgment because no one knows what is best for you, apart from you. "Better" doesn't stop people from needing to wait in long food lines while others have $24,000 freezers stored with food that can easily feed twenty families. There must be a way to build systems for the vast majority of us that are regenerative and sustaining without taking anyone down. Isn't it our time to imagine and write new stories simply because we can?

When we are truly living our best lives, much can happen because there's a knowing inside of us that is dying to create. We'll no longer need to talk about replacing one system with a better one, because we'll be creating systems with integrity and awareness. It can be scary, because it's much easier to remain within the framework and constructs that are familiar—but too often, being safe is way too risky. As we stand at our own intersection, the choices we each make create ripples and are reflected in our collective reality. Is there a way patiently waiting for you to see it?

EXPEDITION 7

LIVING IN POSSIBILITIES

Natural laws are always guiding us to find balance and wholeness. It's in the very design of how we were created. But our societal conditioning has been engineered and hardwired in a way that's not aligned with nature. We've been taught to work against ourselves in unnatural ways. Author Charles Eisenstein reminds us that "when we chop nature into bits in an attempt to understand it, we lose sight of the relationships among those bits. But ecological healing is all about the healing of relationships."

We've been taught to deeply fear death, but life and death are part of our journey. So many try to stay youthful, and yet, aging is a natural process that we've been conditioned to suppress as a way to avoid living fully. When we truly face the fact that one day everything dies, including us, a new desire may spring within us to actually come alive.

Our journey allows us to get closer to who we are and why we're the way we are in our relationships with ourselves, the world, and each other. Just as a violent overthrow of the present regime would not change much of history, it's up to each of us to learn to be gentle with ourselves and deal with our fears. When we have a fear of dying, then we will always have distractions and ways to keep busy so we don't have to think of it. When all we have is a mindset of winning, then we'll always see everyone around us as a competitor we must beat and bring down.

To become whole means to address our deepest wounds and traumas in the depths of our souls. It can't be found externally in a guru, doctor, politician, shaman, celebrity, therapist, lover, supplement, medicine, or diet. It's when we take a deep exploration within ourselves, and observe the pain and hurt we may be suppressing and are not in touch with. Whatever inner work we need is calling us to address it, and to no longer avoid or ignore it. Storms make us stronger and remind us how connected we are to natural cycles. It's time to find our self-compassion and recover our treasures, or continue to fear our very essence. Facing our wounds head-on connects us with the regenerative power of the universe.

Our minds are too often fed fear, which can trigger us to consume more and more. We become so fearful that ultimately, we're giving our power away to a world designed to keep us fighting within ourselves and against each other in a manufactured world of winning at all costs where warriors, heroes, and winners emerge as the main characters carrying the torch of justice and fairness. But what if there's no need to fight or war? What if we can see the battle lines that have been drawn to keep us spinning in stories that don't serve us or the vast majority of humanity?

It's important to keep reminding ourselves that while we don't know for certain who created the Earth and humanity, we do know who created the internet, taxation, government, tiramisu, holidays, petitions, borders, war, and division. And isn't it ironic that many people want to be celebrated with money, status, and attention, and live the illusionary "good life" like the millionaires in our society? What if we simply want to have a meaningful life—one that matters to us and those around us? The current convergence of breakdowns— in finances, politics, education, health, water, soil, the environment, and every other sector of society—is a natural cycle of life and death and an opportunity to shift us from the world of crisis into a healthy one of opportunity and creation. And we can continue to protest and grieve the continued injustice, or those of us who are ready to do our work can come together to imagine, architect and create what is needed most. It's time.

It's Time to Understand What's Natural and What's Unnatural in Our Lives

Can we become aware that we're simply part of nature, and that there is intelligence under our feet with vast networks of plants and trees communicating in community? The birds and the bees need the flowers, and the flowers need the birds and the bees. And our food supply depends on this community playing its natural role. What if we trust the currents and the intelligence that has been waiting for us to see and experience its brilliance? What if we shifted who and what we gave our power to and became aware of what's truly healthy and unhealthy for us? Everything is right here, waiting for us to embody it and reclaim our voices and power, without any judgment. It's simply ready for us to uncover as we become whole and put together our own fragmented pieces like a huge jigsaw puzzle, wanting to create a beautiful mosaic of possibilities.

In other words, there's a way for each of us to allow ourselves to become honest and loving toward ourselves in natural and holistic ways. We're part of a much larger ecosystem. There are fantastic movements emerging in our world to regenerate the planet and how we live collectively—and yet, we first can take a step back and practice setting aside our thinking minds and all of its plans and goals, so we can regenerate ourselves.

Being true to ourselves means that we can go our own way, even when it's at odds with the status quo and the people around us. We can let go of our limitations and preconceived ideas about what is acceptable and what isn't. It's time to become whole and walk our path and align with the creative energy that is our natural birthright.

WHOLENESS IN BODY, MIND, AND SPIRIT

We all desire a certain level of success, advancement, abundance, and fulfilment in our lives, and there's nothing wrong with this. That's all part of our journey. But what we've been conditioned to believe is that the physical and material achievements will bring us true fulfillment. There is always more to have: more fulfillment, more possessions, more recognition. We may find ourselves stuck and attached to the illusion that more and more is the way of life.

To win, we must stand out and make it by being separate from the whole. But we don't have to divide ourselves and keep feeding the machine that has an endless desire to keep us separated and hungry for more. We can become conscious of where our judgment goes, as well as where we choose to invest our own power, our money, and our energy. More divisions and fighting for our lives will not bring unity to our lives or our world. Is our survival dependent on ensuring that we get the carrots, which are dangled in front of us as the ultimate prize, or do we know what's been buried in our hearts—who we are and what we're here to create?

When we create because we feel we're living our purpose, we

care less about making the list and being rewarded and recognized by society. Sure, it's amazing when we are, but winning is not our primary goal. We can still enjoy what we create, and still enjoy the carrot that shows up as a result. *Trekking into the Unknown*, which is the second book in the *F*ck the Bucket List* series, dives more into knowing our "enough" and when enough is enough when it comes to our bodies, minds, and spirits.

A number of small business owners I've met have decided that they no longer want to grow their businesses; the bigger they get, the less time they have to enjoy their lives. And working just to pay higher taxes and manage more people no longer seems appealing—so they've chosen to scale back and understand that they're enough and have what they actually need to live a simple life. And many people today are choosing not to become managers because they don't want to spend their lives managing other adults; we want to practice our art.

The Heart of the Matter

When we're living with the goal of reaching that carrot, we can feel anxiety spreading inside of us. There is an unsettled, stressful feeling that we haven't yet reached our goal. When we focus on a goal that becomes the carrot, it is easy to forget who we are at our core. On this journey, we'll most likely wake up one day and feel exhausted when we realize that we've been chasing something that has always been out of reach.

It happens to all of us—even Nikola Tesla, who shared, "Our first endeavors are purely instinctive prompting of an imagination vivid and undisciplined. As we grow older, reason asserts itself and we become more and more systematic and designing. But those early impulses, though not immediately productive, are of the greatest moment and may shape our very destinies. Indeed, I feel now that had I understood and cultivated instead of suppressing them, I would have added substantial value to my bequest to the world. But not until I had attained manhood did I realize that I was an inventor." Some of us feel despair when we realize that some of our beliefs have jailed us. But this despair is a state of mind. We can free ourselves from our false beliefs when we address our limiting beliefs and societal conditioning.

Knowing what's important to us helps us know who we are and who we are not when we are feeling overwhelmed and confused. It's up to us to assess what is acceptable and unacceptable in our relationships, activities, career, environment, and conversations. We can observe which of our inner thoughts, choices, actions, and feelings are healthy or unhealthy. Once we realize how many unhealthy people and situations we've allowed in our life, we might integrate this practice of self-evaluation.

Have you spent a lifetime accepting unacceptable behavior from others as well as yourself? Do you draw healthy boundaries, and can you see whether a situation is healthy for you or toxic? It may surprise you how often you let unhealthy situations and people in your life.

There's Always a Way

In May 2019 I was invited to a meeting in Washington, DC. When I arrived, I saw that I was the only woman, and one of the organizers told me they wished there were more women in the group—which confused me, because they had invited us and chose who was in the boardroom that day. They could have easily invited anyone they wished.

On the way to dinner after the meeting, one of the organizers asked me if I wanted to know how she described me to people when they asked her about me. "Sure," I said. Claire told me not to take it the wrong way, but she told people that I was a *business hippie.*

"Why?" I asked her, as it was the first time I'd heard this term. She told me it was because I cared about people and talked about collaboration, communication, and conscious leadership. All that apparently made me *hippy-ish* in her eyes, a nonconformist and a troublemaker.

While it made me laugh, I knew not to give energy to continuing the conversation, because that was how she saw me. So I thanked her for sharing her perspective. In my heart, I knew that it was up to me to continue on my path of wanting to create humane systems where people wanted to communicate and create something meaningful together.

Later at the dinner, I sat at a table with four men and started talking to an executive who had recently joined this company's leadership team. We were having an interesting conversation in which he shared his past of being a roadie and an underwear model (he must have heard about me being a "hippie"), when one of the other guys at our table pointed at the two of us and brought us into their "conversation."

He looked at the two other guys at the table and told them that the three of them were privileged white men. "Don't ever forget how privileged you are. And these two"—he pointed to me and the Hispanic man at the table—"know exactly what I mean. It's time for us to be vulnerable and admit that we are." I rubbed my eyes in disbelief that once again I'd heard the words "vulnerability" and "privilege" being spewed so irrationally. For a moment, I forgot about the words and saw how much this man was hurting. He continued to lash out, and one of the guys became increasingly angry, telling him he knew nothing about him. Remember, we had all just met a few hours earlier at a meeting and were now "socializing" at a fancy restaurant in DC.

This evening did not end well, and no matter how hard some of us tried to shift it into a constructive conversation, everyone was so stuck in being right, being vulnerable, and being offended that there was no way out. And apart from declaring the need to be vulnerable, there was no interest in having dialogue to dig beneath the layers of what was really being discussed.

These were very successful men that were hurting. They put on their fancy suits and armor, but you could see that they were going through something themselves and might have something that needed to emerge from all that anger and hurt. It made me sad that one of the guys simply walked out when it got too crazy for him—but it was escalating so much that it could have ended in a fistfight.

It was not my meeting or my place to jump in more than I did. But this is what happened when a nonprofit leader, former tech executive, and a former Harvard professor had dinner in Washington, DC. Many people walking around our planet are at a breaking point and feel unsupported and confused. Many are choosing to leave the planet because they are hurting or have given up. You can call me whatever you want, because I know who I am and what I am about, and what matters most to me is seeing more of us connecting in open dialogue rather than lashing out and standing behind concepts like vulnerability and privilege, creating more division in a divided world. How can anything be created when we are entrenched in destructive belief systems and so desperately need to be seen?

The opportunity is to come together and create healthy stories and understand that we don't have to live in all the hurt and the pain. We will see more of this come up because the skills that are needed for the path forward are ones that bring back our humanity and ability to connect, rather than divide, around the world we truly want to live in. It pains me to include this story in the book, but it is real and raw, and happened a year ago right here, right now. Again, the opportunity is to learn from it and ask questions that open us up to possibilities of creating healthy stories.

Imagine if the five of us had spent our dinnertime in creation energy, where we would have discussed how we could work together and how that would impact the world. So much could have emerged. But everyone has to be ready, and it was obvious here that the pain and divides ran too deep. For me, it was as though someone had just read a book on vulnerability and did not have the skills yet to apply it in the real world. Imagine what would be possible if teachers and educators started preparing our next generation to be the best they could be instead of preparing them for unknown jobs that bring fear and uncertainty into our collective future.

So Much Is Possible When We Start Exploring the Edges

We're born to venture into uncharted territories in search of possibilities. It's a voyage of courage to show up with questions and an imagination. To many of us, business is becoming much more personal, because so much of our trust has been broken as employees, customers, and consumers. Maybe it's time to support the people and organizations creating healthy products and experiences by consciously reimagining where and how we shop, work, and live.

Like many others who have (for a while) thrived inside the walls of corporations, I know that we can do business in much healthier, saner, and more beautiful ways. I even wrote *Our Journey to Corporate Sanity: Transformational Stories from the Frontiers of 21st Century Leadership,* a book with amazing stories of conscious leaders. In some respects, smaller businesses collectively are exerting increasing influence and therefore have increasing responsibility for implementing such transformational shifts in society as well.

When we understand that there is more to life than a job, we can do our own inner work that focuses on our well-being. And when we do, connections will become stronger. We may even spend our energy on ourselves, consuming healthier food, people, and beliefs. We may have more time to enjoy what is here waiting for us to experience it—whether it's hiking in the woods, swimming in the ocean, conversing with interesting people, reading books, playing with kids, experiencing live music, or whatever else brings us closer to joy. However, without healthy organizations serving society's well-being, we'll be compromised by the appetites of private power, shareholder value, and pure greed.

Creating a healthy, humane world requires more than new organizational models that shift the deck chairs on a sinking ship. It takes entirely reimagining the nature of business, work, and life. We can no longer afford to separate work and life into two neat boxes, or segment organizations into distinct internal functions that fight each other for budgets and resources. While many antiquated practices still exist, it's becoming more and more urgent to leave them behind and discover healthier paths forward. We can choose to stop believing the myth that change can only come from the top of the organization, because we live in a more open and connected world where there is an increase in transparency of communication.

Our economic and business markets have been created and based on scarcity, but information is abundant. Many organizations talk about innovation but when we actually look at their strategies, we find their growth comes from acquiring smaller, innovative companies. The result of modern-day innovation is tech giant monopolies that each of us is supporting through our consumption. While this is happening on a scale not seen in the past two hundred years, it cannot last because the most basic need of humanity is to freely exchange ideas.

What is emerging cannot be easily found in the mainstream media and information sources. We have to be curious and look for this information to see how people like you and me are reimagining our lives. I remember reading about a grassroots nonprofit in Greece that mapped the country's food co-ops, alternative producers, parallel currencies, and local exchange systems, and ended up uncovering hundreds of small initiatives ranging from carpools to free kindergartens. To mainstream economics, such things seem barely to qualify as economic activity—but that's the point. They exist because they trade—however haltingly and inefficiently—in the currency of free time, networked activity, and free stuff. They created an entire alternative to a global system, but so did money and credit in the age of King Edward III.

With an opportunity mindset, you can discover unique opportunities to create new markets, products, services, and, most importantly, meaningful experiences for people. As people make different choices or stand up for ourselves, healthier paths for living and working will emerge. As fewer of us follow the noise of what is expected of us and instead follow our intuition, we will begin to trust it to guide us in new ways.

Change to the Current World Order Will Only Come from Within Us

Change will only come when we become more aware of the practices of organizations and people we bring into our lives. Making healthier choices is the most important job we will ever have in our lifetimes, as we get closer to navigating our own compasses. When we become aware that we can write the rules for ourselves, much can shift. Here is some food for thought about changing the game you may find yourself in:

1. When the cards are stacked against you, you are set up to lose. In a winner-takes-all world, you can either lose, move to the next game, or step out of the game.

2. When the game is fixed or you don't agree with the rules of the game, decide whether you're all the way in or all the way out.

3. When you understand the rules of the game, but you no longer want to follow them because there's something inherently unhealthy about them, you can invent your own. In a healthy world, it should not be necessary for others to lose in order for you to win. What are some examples of ways you can lift yourself and others up without taking anybody else down? How can you commit to simply be the best you can be without having to compare yourself to anyone else?

It's no longer just the responsibility of corporations and governments, or their leaders, to effect the change we want to see in our lives and world. When we become the leaders of our own lives by making healthy choices for ourselves, we can then find ways to bring people together to create something meaningful in the world. One of the most important skills that conscious leaders have is the ability to listen and have empathy. You are able to take on the current challenges with a mindset of opportunity, and no longer see your work as just a job or a title. What opportunities might emerge if you tapped into your compassion and empathy and started truly creating shared purpose around every part of your work?

There is another way to tell the story of our world, and that canvas is fresh and ready for healthy artists. Let's celebrate our ability to imagine being the impetus for human and planetary balance and sustainability. The expeditions in this book have been filled with questions for the explorer and adventurer, and I hope that they have helped guide you to customize your own journey through a world of possibilities toward our collective sanity.

WHAT HAPPENS WHEN WE HAVE NOTHING TO LOSE?

Architect, inventor, and philosopher Buckminster (Bucky) Fuller—in a rare interview that was recently discovered and posted online—shared that at the age of thirty-two he decided to start thinking for himself. He decided to rely on his current experiences as his guide. He then chose to remain silent, as he'd begun to realize the importance of sounds and words, and how so much of what was being expressed around him consisted of clichés or someone else's beliefs. There was an artificial politeness in how people greeted each other that showed him that most people put on a façade to hide what was really happening in their lives.

He was married and penniless, and he realized that all his contemporaries were focused on making a living. In 1927, after attempting to make a life in construction, he lost all his money and the capital his friends had invested with him. The experience led him to conclude that he was a failure when it came to making a living.

With a wife and a newborn daughter, he found himself broke, unemployed, and undeserving of credit. Feeling hopeless about being able to provide for his family, he decided to commit suicide so his wife could live off his life insurance policy. While standing on a cliff above Lake Michigan, ready to jump to his death, he had an epiphany that changed the course of his life and the lives of many others: "In committing suicide, I seemingly would never again have to feel the pain and mortification of my failures and errors, but the only-by-experience-winnable inventory of knowledge that I had accrued would also be forever lost—an inventory of information that, if I did not commit suicide, might prove to be of critical advantage to others, possibly to all others, possibly to Universe."

He decided to steer his ship into uncharted waters by discovering his own path. "If I take oath never again to work for my own advantage and to work only for all others for whom my experience-gained knowledge may be of benefit, I may be justified in not throwing myself away. This will, of course, mean that I will not be able to escape the pain and mortification of being an absolute failure in playing the game of life as it has been taught to me."

Bucky realized that he was not a spectator of the world, because he could predict how the world could evolve. It gave him the courage to be an independent thinker, uninfluenced by what people wanted him to think. To do so, he became aware that he had to move away from everything he was taught to believe, which was simply part of the game. He stopped accepting beliefs about physical phenomena that were not proven and tested. For example, he noticed that when someone said "hello" to somebody else, the other would say "hi" back, and there was a sort of parrot game going on without either party ever caring how the other was feeling. He became increasingly aware of conditioned patterns and stopped talking altogether.

His intuition whispered to him to find new ways to create success for all of humanity, because if you don't think about the collective, all of humanity will be in real trouble. No one else was attending to what was possible; they were focused on division and survival, creating a "them" and "us" mindset that thrived on conflict and war. He found most countries and politicians were looking out for themselves and no one was looking out for the "Spaceship Earth," a term he invented, since he believed humans were put on this spaceship with resources and know-how to take care of everybody onboard. Maybe Bucky was the original business hippie?

At thirty-two, his life expectancy at the time was forty-two, and he realized the way we were designed is a consequence of the biosphere of this planet. We breathe the air because it is available, and yet some of us hoard as much money as we can get our hands on. He decided to take part in nature's own creation by building bridges for all humanity in the ten years he had with the tools he was given. He knew that all ecology was inner-supportive, regenerative, and effective, and he wanted to tap into this universal intelligence. "You have to learn over and over that you are a no one. Be preoccupied with the possibility. Forget the problem and instead construct."

You don't have to know anything to criticize, judge, or blame (being negative), but it takes a lot to see the opportunity of creation, which is where he focused. He saw that most governments, politicians, religious leaders, and corporations were focused on humanity's suffering. He had hope in young people, and people who want to live in harmony with the universe and nature. He felt he had nothing to lose as he saw himself as a throw-away.

Humanity has another option and is in the "final exam" of whether people are aware of what we can create. Our path is invisible, as it has not been taken before but is based on the regenerative integrity of the universe. People won't use the bridge if we don't know it's there. Bucky focused on his creations through his artifacts, creating geodesic dome structures and writing books rather than focusing on social reform. The money he raised went mostly for research, and he wanted people to create and stay humble. "The only way you ever learn anything is by daring to be naive."

Without marketing or public relations campaigns, Buckminster Fuller was mentioned in over 100,000 books, articles, and broadcasts.

He circled the globe forty-seven times in the last twenty years of his life, published twenty-four books, and funneled twenty million dollars into prototyping and designing of dozens of artifacts—from domes to cars to prefab bathrooms. Though his annual earnings eventually came to $250,000, he spent every dollar on research and development, "always operating in proximity to bankruptcy without going bankrupt."

Bucky died at the age of eighty-eight—forty-six years more years than expected. His voice lives on to help us steer Spaceship Earth in a healthy direction for the collective, and to teach us there is nothing to lose when you follow your internal compass and never give up.

ISN'T IT TIME TO RECLAIM YOUR POWER?

"More is better" is the motto of our day, as well as mantras like "new and improved." Who in their right mind wants to be seen with old and decaying stuff? Our kids are raised around the latest trends, and they often get bullied when they are not dressed in the latest fashions—including having the best and latest technology. We have created a consumer culture that is based on the fast-food model. In our growing addiction to busyness, we have disconnected from the natural cycles of life, establishing our primary goal as consumption when the opportunity, like with Bucky Fuller, is to create. Giving up is easy, while sticking to creating something from your imagination is not.

You can make healthier choices and take action to become the creator of your life rather than a puppet or a victim in someone else's story. You may feel bound by certain circumstances or beliefs, but this could be simply because you have not invested in sufficiently examining and challenging your beliefs. I found it helpful to pose a few what-if scenarios to see where the answers would take me. What if I did not let go and trust the currents? What's the worst thing that could happen? What if I didn't start questioning everything? What if there is another way?

No one else will do it for you. This is your life, and how it plays out is up to you. Are you conscious of the decisions you make regarding where you shop, where you eat, what you consume, what you watch, who you spend time with, and, most importantly, where you work and how you define yourself?

We have been conditioned to hold back from what is abundant on our planet. As the doors are opening, it's up to each of us to take the first step to a healthy life by letting go of false ideals designed to keep us safe. The love that we deserve most comes from deep within us. When we can love our perceived imperfections, and see our mistakes simply as lessons, we can experience self-love—and then bring this deep love into our world through imagination, courage, and knowing that there is another organic, healthy way for us to create on this planet. When we imagine what's actually possible to be present with ourselves, we will become aware that we don't all need a bucket list to live our lives for *someday*.

It would be a sad and defeated world that simply accepted the status quo. The current state of endless financial growth, at the expense of people and the planet, can shift. It does not need to be upgraded or transformed—it needs for you to imagine what else is possible, beyond the current status quo. There are plenty of options available, but they take action, dialogue, connection, and thoughtful creation. The mind of an artist and creator is needed instead of looking at the same piece of art and trying to only make it "better," more "innovative," or "improve" upon it. Letting go means making space for your wildest creations.

Of course, transcending systems might feel impossible to you right now. The mainstream has its feet firmly planted and deeply rooted in that soil and is spreading the toxic beliefs through its underground roots. Our world does not need more outrage and fear marching through our streets and the dark hallways of our minds. It is time to enlighten people to the depth of what is possible. Instead of fighting and warring and creating more division, the opportunity is to break away from the mob mentality and simply create with courage at a healthy speed. John F. Kennedy's words continue to guide us, "Let us not despair but act … Let us not seek to fix the blame for the past—let us accept our own responsibility for the future."

The path to a healthier world is being paved by curious and imaginative people who are brave enough to acknowledge that the wisdom we received from our schools, our ancestors, and our governments is no longer working and is at death's door. It's time to design the systems you need with fresh eyes and an open heart. Who? You? Yes, you! When you are ready, thank your ancestors for bringing you here, but you no longer need to be burdened by what doesn't work. They want you to let go so they can rest in peace and allow you the freedom to create through trial and error, until our individual and collective bodies, minds, and souls are thriving in harmony with life itself. There is no need for utopia or perfection, just a healthy desire to create a healthier reality.

When we choose to stay in our cave, more comfortable with the shadows on the wall, closely protecting ourselves, we will be experiencing life in the cave and its surroundings. That is all we will know. We will most likely not want to hear about opportunities or become aware that there is another way, and a world waiting to be created. This book is for those who never give up. Because you know that nothing meaningful ever comes too easily.

The way forward is to go inside ourselves and choose not to go down fear-based rabbit holes. It's personal to find our wonder and awe, trek into the unknown, and trust our hearts.

Stand firm and grounded while opening your heart. It's our time to let our light shine and create the world we choose to live in.

EXPEDITION 8

DISCOVER THE WONDER OF YOU

What if we can live a joyful life and be ourselves in a world that's constantly trying to make us be like everyone else? When we can't be ourselves and express who we really are, life usually gets very challenging—like when we're playing a role that doesn't represent who we are at our core, working a job that pays the bills but fails to fulfill our soul, staying in hurtful relationships, or living a lifestyle that is at odds with our values. But how do we know what's healthy or unhealthy for us unless we experience life to the fullest?

The greatest delusion we may be experiencing is that we are powerless to deal with the overwhelming darkness that is going on in our world. And nothing could be further from the truth. The noise of this world can be deafening and distracting. You'll be overwhelmed, stressed, or simply living in fear—all weakening your immune system. It can be scary or exciting not to know where you're headed, but you're more in control than you ever imagined. The question is, what is within your control and what do you imagine as your journey—not your destination? Maybe it's an ability to trust yourself enough to steer toward what truly ignites your soul. Maybe, like Bucky Fuller, you realize that "you never change things by fighting the existing reality. To change something, build a new model that makes the existing model obsolete."

We don't need to be victims of false identities and stories. There were generations of children who played outdoors and would find themselves lying on the grass, curious about what lay beyond the horizon, imagining possibilities. Parents often complain that their kids cannot detach from their devices and have no interest in going outside. Is it because of devices that our kids have become separated from nature?

It is not the technology itself that is to blame. For those ingrained in our current paradigms of how we are supposed to live and work, and what's appropriate and inappropriate (another version of right and wrong), there's no space or time to imagine. It's not that our kids don't want to play outside because of technology—it's that the programming we are running on keeps them as busy and distracted as we are. Like us, they get their cues from what is valued, rewarded, and recognized in the external world as we encourage them to be responsible and grow up. Our own level of play and playfulness teaches them, as well as our own relationship with life.

Sovereignty comes from within. When we shift from fighting and start flowing with the natural currents and rhythm of life, we'll discover what has been waiting for us. The decaying paradigms of competition will no longer be effective when we shift to rely on our own power source. Until we take bold steps into the unknown, the status quo will continue to be deafening with more conflicts, pain, and deep division. More of the same is more of the same. The only way out is in. And yet the virus of fear keeps us haunted by our own shadows. Why take anyone down in a world that has a twisted version of justice and fairness playing out in reality? Why compete to be *the* superstar when we can co-create? Let's be mindful of our conditioning of believing we should live as winners, unconscious of what we're actually losing.

A CALL TO ACTION

Sometimes life shows us that having to make do with less is a gift. This is what happened to many people during the spring of 2020, when we found ourselves with nowhere to go unless we were essential workers. Many found this period of time incredibly uncomfortable, as the comfort of having a busy life filled with nonstop activities came to a standstill. There was literally nowhere to go, and the stress of this new reality was not appreciated by those of us who fed ourselves with always being in motion. The frequent fliers were asked to stay home, and our train stations, highways, and airports became hauntingly still. We could not hug each other or be close to the dying when they took their last breath. We waited until we couldn't anymore. One crisis turned into another and the images from the protests in Hong Kong, across the US, and in other parts of the world reminded us of the pictures we had seen only in historical movies or books. The deep divides, injustices, agendas, power struggles and societal depression played out on our screens and streets.

But maybe less activity and racing around from point A to point B allowed us more time for connection and conversation, even with ourselves. For many of us, it was scary to be still and have time to think. Every day we were bombarded with more external information and theories to occupy our minds—and many just wanted to know when we would be *allowed* to get back to our normal, busy lives.

But the truth of the matter is that this was the first time we all had a front row seat to the lack of leadership in our world in every sector—from business, to politics, to education, to health care—despite all the *Harvard Business Review* case studies, the top leadership lists, and awards. We didn't dare say it out loud, but more and more of us realized that no one knows much of anything. We may have even realized that less mass media and theories bring us more awareness of our opportunities to trust ourselves and listen deeply to what our souls are whispering to us. Less noise, more peace? Maybe we could actually get used to less noise and more connection to ourselves, each other, and nature?

Observations and Insights from Fellow Humans

I believe that we are all connected, so below I share with you the thoughts of fellow humans that have sparked me. The only one I've met in person is Seth Godin, and the rest are fellow humans I connected with online by reading their posts. But at some point, our work is all connected, and all that is needed are bridges and architects to emerge together. Imagine if all the people working in isolation on creating the next generation of regenerative agriculture, humane business, education, health care, economics, political and legal systems came together to co-create with kindness, compassion, and deep meaning. Now more than ever, the next big wave is not some human-imagined technology but humanity itself.

Fellow human Jason Hine shared on his page, "Some folks are now trying to design open source ventilators, some are providing food to older people, some are protecting fragile people, some are digging their gardens to grow food, some are connecting more deeply to the earth . . . Some are going deeper into ritual to work with viruses, some are reading multiple scientific papers, some are staring down a microscope, some are engaging in activism . . . Some are gathering herbs, some are designing new economic systems, some are struggling in difficult or painful circumstances, some are providing comfort for those who are struggling.

"All of these responses are valid. What is important is perhaps this: When the time came, the world turned and things began to fall apart, did you fight imaginary enemies, or did you stand up? Now your true character will be revealed. Did you arrive? Did you do those sacred tasks which you know you have to do? Did you do those things which were given to you by some invisible power or by your soul or by your conscience? Did you do that which you know you have to do: did you do what you must? Did you listen to the call? Did you turn up? Did you report to do what you are here to do?"

Fellow human Micheila Sheldan writes, "We are entering uncharted territory and it's going to require reaching way outside the box to reclaim our freedom, tearing our false safety nets to shreds. But once those nets are gone, we will realize just how free we've been all along . . . and exactly where our personal truths lie."

Fellow human Seth Godin provides this insight: "So what's next? A commitment to learning and to possibility. The pandemic demonstrated, among other things, that we all have access to each other digitally. That if you want to learn something, the chance is there. That internet connections can be powerful, and that leadership is priceless. The industrial era, struggling for the last decade or two, is now officially being replaced by one based on connection and leadership and the opportunity to show up and make a difference."

Fellow human Joe Brewer shared, "Yesterday I felt a deep stirring of emotions . . . a pattern was visible of people becoming unsettled in this moment of the evolutionary process. I held sadness and pain.

Grief and trauma. Love and fear. Judgment and broken discernment. It was in the air I breathed and could be felt palpably among those I interacted with. This has continued into the morning while I put together the final slides for my webinar today. In six hours, I will give a talk to more than 100 people sharing case studies in real-world bioregional regeneration. The content gathered to share in this presentation shows what is emerging to compost the collapse of the globalized economy. None of the bioregions is functionally healthy or free from the shackles of this larger system that is in the process of dying around them.

"Yet if you squint your eyes you can see the contours of the future emerging. The portion of humanity that survives this century will be rooted in these places; grounded in living systems; sharing the stewardship of healing landscapes. Today I will present examples of rust belt cities reinventing themselves; fisheries that collapsed and are now being managed more thoughtfully; river valleys being nurtured back to life; children being raised in right relationships with their landscapes; and it is all beautiful. My heart remains open and I continue to feel the waves of change flowing through me and around me. I will not flinch or close my body to the sensations. For these emotions are my compass telling me where to take my next step.

"Onward, fellow humans."

Are You Curious Enough to Take Your Next Step?

Will we go on suffering through life being busy and occupied with how life should be, or will we let the light in and choose to create something outside of this decaying paradigm, which no longer resonates with who we are? How do we unwind from limiting beliefs that constrain our very being? Can we take steps outside of our comfort zones when we become aware that the safety nets are no longer safe for us?

Often, being safe is very risky. There are so many opportunities when we let go of the notion of comfort and safety—not in blame or shame, as that will keep us stuck in the dying paradigm. We can shift our energy to become comfortable with the unknown and reignite our curiosity, especially in challenging times. We can shift to currencies and systems that serve the vast majority of humanity, like trust, relationships, and community. What messages are coming to you every day? Are they healthy for you? What are you communicating to yourself about what's going on in the world? Is it fear-based? What are you creating for yourself every day? Can you be still and listen deeply to your heartbeat? When we're living in fear, we don't have the capacity to connect with ourselves or each other. What conversations are you having with yourself and with others? Make space to find out, as it impacts your immunity and health.

When we become immersed in the projection of what will happen in the future based on what happened in the past, we're recreating the past whether it's our health, our relationships, or our job. No one knows what will happen tomorrow. Everyone is guessing and making it up. It's just that those we give our power to seem to have also been given the power to tell us how the world works. The truth of the matter is that no one is coming to save us, because we don't need to be saved. One of the first steps we can take is becoming conscious of who and what we give our power to, and why, because it matters.

Can you give up on the current idea of control, safety, and comfort? That's what trekking into the unknown is all about. We're here in one of the most transformational times in human history. Can you live in mystery, or just watch it on TV or on a screen? What's taking place now on our planet is people trying to hang on to power with false hope. Who holds our sovereignty to transform basic foundational paradigms? And when will we let go and find each other to create what's possible? Old paradigms are running on life support. When do we unplug and plug into our power source?

Are you in contact with your authentic self? That is the communication to focus on when you stop being busy crossing items off your list and adding new ones. Are you in tune with yourself and your own knowing? Do you understand the programs running through your mind? This is a pivotal time to do our "work" individually and collectively. I can see when people hear what I'm saying, but some part of them resists it because it forces them to address something deep inside. Feel the resistance in your body to see the parts of you that need attention and healing.

Everything that's becoming unstable is part of a paradigm that can't uphold the inequalities of our separation from ourselves, each other, and nature. It's time to raise the bar on what we actually need, in balance, and not rely on what we've been told to consume. No competition or suppression is needed.

Do you realize that you're here to bring joy and fulfillment, or did you come here to fear and suffer? You're the authority that regulates how you respond and react. Our current systems—like what we call leadership—are crumbling. What can you release so you can create?

Operating in the field of the unknown relies on the knowing, as things that have been taken away are restored, but in different ways. The new can't come in when we stay focused on the past. Make space. Take time. Release what is anchored in the past to live in possibilities.

No one knows what the future will hold. Find comfort in whatever the future brings; there will be opportunities when we remain open, curious, and roll up our sleeves to blaze with a ton of deep knowing that there's always a way for powerful creators to co-create new, healthy systems.

All it takes in this moment is being the doorway and the bridge for others to walk through. If you're a parent, be that humane leader for your kids. Inner authenticity cannot be seen by others; it's a practice that shines through you. We're meant to use our inner guidance to navigate through this time. People respond immediately when there's a collective fear for our health or anything challenging us. What if we created in response to our biggest opportunities? What would we be creating? We are so powerful, but we simply forgot.

When our hearts are not into something, we can either find a way to ignite our passionate hearts, or let stuff go. Are you saying yes to someone when you'd prefer to say no? Could that someone be yourself? The sooner you recognize this, the sooner you'll recover a sense of freedom and joy.

ATTITUDE IS THE KEY TO PRETTY MUCH EVERYTHING

There is freedom in the attitude we choose to adopt—it can free us or imprison our soul. Our attitude determines how we communicate with ourselves, the type of people we attract into our lives, and how we're treated once we're aware of the role trauma and pain play in our lives. Recognizing and dealing with our difficulties takes courage. There's no universal formula for how we address it. But attitude determines the state of our health and well-being, because self-love can do more for us than a judgmental, angry, or cynical attitude. Where can you tweak your attitude and let your kindness shine?

Become clear on where your thinking may be falling short and letting you down. There are times in life when our attitudes are less than perfect. We might experience a bout of cynicism or anger, believing we're not good enough, or feeling sad or disconnected because of pain from our past. When we live in awareness, we can weed out negative energy so we can make the most of aligning our life.

No one else can tell us what's best for us. People can sometimes see little nuggets of truth about us and deliver accurate insights. Only you can discover your essence—the core of who you really are. The best way to uncover your core is to engage in moments of transcendence— perhaps when you sing, dance, draw, or commune with nature. You have the opportunity to get a little closer to understanding who you are and discovering the wonder of you. When do you forget time and all your worries? When do you experience a sense of connection and peace? When are you most joyful? It's up to you to discover your pathway opening that leads to joy, when you are brave enough to explore yourself.

Inner harmony comes from seeing life as one big adventure, otherwise we will be spinning our wheels chasing someone else's dream. Imagination is crucial to finding ways to play outside the boxes of conformity. However, it still challenges those who function behind the invisible bars and man-made prisons of the mind, as they have a great need to organize and pigeonhole everyone into neat little boxes in order to understand and operate from *their* box.

Consciously creating fun and play in your world probably goes against everything you learned in your upbringing. Especially if you were taught to win at all costs to be successful. If this is the case, maybe now is a good time to revisit the "manual" you were given and consider coloring outside of the lines.

BEING YOUR OWN GUIDE

We learn through our experiences. We can read, we can talk, we can listen, we can exchange ideas, we can be entertained, we can play. But to truly become aware of what is healthy or unhealthy for us, we must address our limiting beliefs and tap into our curiosity and humility. I've shared with you some of my limiting beliefs and conditioning, which I continue to work through, as there's no quick switch to flip to become aware of how they're manifesting in my life.

When we become aware and conscious of our limiting beliefs, labels, and rationalizations of how life is supposed to be, we can observe ourselves by questioning everything. It's our own life of exploration to discover, so we can lighten the weight of the baggage we carry around with us every moment of the day. Sitting back and observing allows us to hear and locate our wounds and traumas, and also our gifts. Connecting to nature can override so much and holds the greatest power to govern us in alignment with the natural world that we're part of. It's up to us to understand that unity, not conformity or uniformity, is the bridge of separation and division.

What does this mean? It means that when we see our internal conflicts and deep divisions or voices that are fighting within us, we can give them names and become aware of where they originate and whether we want to hold on to them. Then, to become whole, we can uncover creative ways to integrate them. What practices we bring in is personal for each of us, since no one else can do this for us. And it's very personal as there's no one-size-fits-all, which is part of the dying paradigm. For some, it may include reflection and resting of the body and mind, and for others it could be journaling or therapy.

As we've been discussing throughout this experience, your attitude and mindset hold the key to your health. So much suffering in life comes from wishing things were different, so when you can't change a situation, maybe you can look for the lesson behind it or see whether you can uncover the root cause. As the saying goes, if life gives you lemons, make lemonade. A willingness to let go and surrender to whatever happens is one way forward, and seeing the opportunity in a difficult situation can make the difference between suffering and living in your own way.

In this world full of experts telling us what's what but often not agreeing and creating battle zones, the healthiest course of action, especially when you're not sure about something, is to trust your intuition. Whether it's a feeling you have deep in your bones or whispers in your gut, trust it. One thing we know for sure is that it's unlikely that things will run smoothly, so you might need to let go of something (and let it die) or embrace a new beginning. This is a time of opportunity—a potential healthy chapter of your life. You might be questioning your general direction in life, and it's up to you to decide when you're consciously ready to step into your power. Perhaps it's a case of sorting out your foundations, and then you'll find it easier to take big steps forward in the outside world.

One of the many crazy things I did when I started my journey was to enter a partnership with people who had created a practice around what they called "shadow work" and dreamed of creating a modern-day philosopher's bootcamp and mystery school like the ones of the ancients. What I didn't know was that their process was a deeply painful process—one I hope no one else will have to experience—and what I learned firsthand was to trust myself. There is no one outside ourselves who holds our answers, and what may be healthy for someone else is often unhealthy for us. The mirror they put up for me to see myself also reflected the brokenness within all of us, and it showed me that we all have work to do. The only way to know is to experiment with no regrets.

There were some useful kernels that I did integrate from this experience, but I also promised myself to be more discerning about the people I bring into my life and to observe whether they practice what they preach. Some of the stuff they did behind closed doors was insane, but it did end up pushing me away from them in a healthier direction of needing to do meaningful work in our world. It means being truly seen and heard, listening deeply, connecting, playing, loving and being loved, exploring the edges, and having adventures that serve something bigger than myself. Additional partnerships came to test me along the path, and it was a way to practice whether the people I was letting into my heart were healthy for me, and acknowledging that everyone is simply doing their best.

BECOMING A BEACON OF LOVE

Living in a rain forest taught me the beauty of integration as I learned how fierce nature is, which was quite different than what I had been taught. I've seen a whole different side of birds—for example, crows and ravens attacking bald eagles over food, safety, and security. I learned that it's perfectly okay to accomplish absolutely nothing and live in harmony. When I used to go on trips to Tahoe, we would fear the bears. Now, I spend hours watching the bears come out of the forest (at a safe distance) and I simply observe their energy and curiosity, especially the cubs. I'm able to see how self-sufficient the animals and plants around me are, and the natural laws that govern us, like flow and unity. And it's also not always calm and rosy, as the seasons and circumstances change constantly.

Listening to the tracks running through our mind—even our unnatural separation from nature—allows us to become more aware of our unhealthy programming and begin taking action. For me, no longer sucking up in failed relationships was a big deal, since I found abundant joy in being still and integrating my internal power source, as well as not needing to numb myself with activities and accomplishments. On this journey, doing extensive research on "reality" and finding shocking information on people I trusted was devastating but necessary. I started to see with healthy eyes what was hidden from me in full sight.

Much of it was about the power structures we've created in the world: mind control, military force, surveillance, censorship, media control, and the use of technologies that keep us locked in a scarcity mindset. What we've been led to believe is progress and innovation is simply a delusion, as most of the systems in place continue to serve only those with the most power. Most of the money in the world is held by the few who have an insatiable need to amass more and more, and to do so they simply need us to tune in to their programming, obey their rules, and continue to consume in the name of progress. But this is a time not just to learn but to act, as Aldous Huxley shares: "That men do not learn very much from the lessons of history is the most important of all the lessons that history has to teach."

Each of us can find our own path in our own way—and when someone is struggling, we can listen and not jump to solving problems, but rather to finding bridges to lift each other up. When someone is lost in confusion, we can listen, and when appropriate, share our perspective with no attempt to convert them to our way of thinking. When we see someone spinning in a maze, feeling there is no way out, we can listen even more and hold them in our hearts— especially when we're not *allowed* to hug or touch each other, as in the case of COVID-19 in 2020.

When we realize that imprisoning our souls in suffering is optional, we can face our shadows and ancestral imprints, which requires us to navigate through layers of pain, sadness, anger and fear. We can then commit to discovering our awe, without the need to bring shame or judgment along. For me, facing my darkness released my attachments to stories, people, beliefs, and food that were toxic. It also allowed me to learn to assess relationships faster and walk away when my intuition signaled to me that one was unhealthy. No matter how much my soul was longing to find that spark of connection to co-create, I learned to discern when I was doing it at my own expense—and remembered there are close to eight billion people on the planet, which gives me plenty of opportunities to connect.

We're at a major intersection right now, and we were born for this time when we embrace our sovereignty. It's a matter of unlearning and un-conditioning from toxic beliefs and practices that have been ingrained in us as we choose trust and embrace our own authenticity, compassion, integrity, and love of ourselves. The results are different for each of us, and that's the point. We don't need to save the world or make it better. We only accelerate things for humanity and the planet when we first liberate ourselves. Where does your freedom lie?

EXPEDITION 9

THE END AS THE BEGINNING

hank you for being on this journey; it's one with a lot of places to visit and decisions to make for yourself. It takes a lot of curiosity, creativity, and courage to explore ourselves from the inside out. Despite the state of our world and economies right now, I'm extremely hopeful, even optimistic, that this is one of the biggest opportunities to build the bridges we need to a healthier life, individually and collectively.

What got us here will no longer take us where we're headed, and that is scary for a lot of us who want to hang on to our perceived comfort and safety. We each have the same opportunity to come face-to-face with the illusions and delusions we were brought up with and to practice how to walk toward our own path. The only way to get there is to take the first step, in your own way, by tuning down the volume, noise, or entity that tries to control you. It's about becoming aware of your relationship with fear, money, nature, work, safety, social status, people, ourselves, and life itself. Self-love is not narcissism, as all you ever want to be is the best and healthiest version of yourself, no strings attached. When we realize we are not separate from nature, we understand how interconnected we have always been.

As we were initiated into this journey in the beginning of the book, we were reminded that good and bad, right and wrong are constructs that we inherited and that may no longer serve us in their current form. As Rosamund Stone Zander shared in *The Art of Possibility*, "The rain in Florida may be bad for us and good for the citrus crop. A canceled flight may wreck our schedule and bring us face to face with our future spouse in the airport lounge. A forest fire may seem to destroy an ecosystem in the short term, yet renew it with vigor for the long term. When a splendid osprey eats a beautiful fish, it is neither good nor bad. Or, it's good for the osprey and bad for the fish. Nature makes no judgment. Humans do." Imagine that you can discover your own way to living a healthy life.

OBSERVATIONS ALONG THE PATH

A lot of people are struggling right now, as uncertainty continues to rear its head around us. We haven't seen anything yet, as we're in the eye of the storm. I am ending this first book with some observations, and I invite you to begin by setting your own boundaries and making your own realizations and commitments.

Let's dive in . . .

(1) What we give attention to not only matters, but is foundational to discovering our own wonder and awe.

We were never truly separate from nature and never can be, but the dominant culture on earth has long imagined itself to be separate from nature and destined, one day, to transcend it. We have lived in a mythology of separation that continues to be handed over from one generation to the next with an agenda to keep us divided and fighting each other, and ourselves, until we choose to break these cycles, both individually and collectively.

When we meet our personal history with resistance, we stay stuck in our old stories, beliefs, and paradigms. We set up a chain of events with preconceived beliefs and outcomes. We've been taught to look outside ourselves for some standard and norm. We too often meet suffering and resistance in our paths, and fail to recognize that we can also clear them by learning to let go and surrender. We have an ability to see opportunities as much as challenges and problems. We have an opportunity to stay in the present moment by meeting our challenges in healthier ways and understanding our deep attachments. Do you know how to stay in the present moment with what is? Can you learn to let go of the need to control or define your life as rigidly as before?

When you struggle and fight, you're directed away from your alignment and balance. Your energy gets trapped in the good fight. But when you let go of the restricting definitions, suffering, and the need to be a warrior out to battle, your energy gets released to consider opportunities and what you can create with the unique gifts you bring to the planet.

There are multiple challenges that humanity has faced throughout time, but our opportunity is to meet problems with a healthy outlook. The history of war repeats itself constantly across the globe; hardly any place has been left untouched by its destructive power. In our schools, war is taught and reinforced as part of our history curriculum. But it is the fear of a war happening again and again in our lifetime that strengthens its unconscious force within us.

But what if our history classes shared stories of times of peace, of neighbors supporting each other and people collaborating together around a shared purpose? Imagine rewriting our textbooks and giving as much focus and attention to stories of harmony. Let's even imagine tuning in to television, shows, films, plays and documentaries without soldiers, murders, serial killers, sociopaths, pedophiles, adulterers, heroes, or backstabbers. How much energy do we give to the mistakes and points of shame and disappointment in our lives, reliving them again and again in our minds and feeling their pain over and over, and how much attention do we give to moments of joy and play? What is our foundation built on, and what is in alignment? What is out of balance, and why?

Whatever we reinforce in our perception reflects back to us in some way, and that's what can start to change for each of us. There are pioneers like Michael Strong who are building a new wave of education with schools where children have a voice. Michael understands that the next generations will need more experiential skills than our traditional education systems offer.

Michael wants us to imagine and reimagine through his work and writing: "Suppose there was a cabal of evil geniuses who decided to force teens into labor camps where 56% were disengaged, 75% had negative feelings, 17% had to be put on psychiatric medications to survive, suicides had increased 300% since the founding of the labor camp system, and there was an annual 20% increase in suicides each fall when they were forced back into the camps. If this was an Apple factory in China, there would be international protests and boycotts. When it was discovered they were actually doing this to children, the company would collapse. But of course this is exactly what our schooling system does day in, day out, to our teens. It is unconscionable by any human standard.

"While the need for greater access to mental health resources is certainly urgent, I want readers to take another possibility seriously: Perhaps a re-examination of the institution of schooling is even more urgent. If our existing schooling system is unnecessarily exacerbating mental health issues, then parents, teens, educators, and policy-makers should re-evaluate the premises of our existing schooling system. If schooling-as-we-know-it is excessively different from our environment of evolutionary adaptation, then how should we rethink schooling in order to create healthier adolescent populations in the future?"

If you're curious enough to learn more, reach out to Michael and connect with him, as he is creating a game plan for how to develop greater awareness and healthier pathways for teens.

To truly create a healthy world, our fundamental systems need to adapt and work in healthy and peaceful ways. Imagine history classes focusing on ancient indigenous civilizations where women sat around the fire making daily decisions as a community. Do we want to focus on solving humanity's biggest problems, which anchors us in the past, or do we want to trek into the unknown and be curious about our biggest opportunities, individually and collectively?

Whenever we are strengthening a belief or statement, we have the ability to anchor in a reality we don't desire. When we hate or fear someone or something, the more attention we give to blaming them for our circumstances, the more we keep this story alive. If we're constantly stating that we don't consent to something we don't want, we're actually strengthening it by giving it our attention. For example, when we get caught up in how someone has wronged us and talk about it all the time with whoever will listen, we're reinforcing our reality to bring us more experiences like this until we're ready to become aware and break the pattern. Constant outrage and blame no longer bring us healthy outcomes unless we break the pattern of winning at all costs and our ego's insatiable need to be right.

Breaking free is possible. Everything is imprinted by a story, experience, and energy. This is why examining our beliefs and conditioning is so important for us to discover our own wonder. It may require us to spend time alone or make time to be still so we can recalibrate the navigation system within us to who we're becoming.

(2) Our MINDSET is everything!

Anyone can mouth words and provide insight, just as anyone can bake by following a recipe, or repeat the moves of a golfer. It is the mindset and energy of the master black belt that makes the skill and wisdom powerful. Mindset is the way you think, and the way you perceive the world, and how you interpret events in your world. The healthiest way to shift a pattern starts with becoming aware of the pattern.

When our minds are filled with negative beliefs and thoughts, we get stuck in a never-ending cycle of problems as we see the world through this lens. The human brain has been wired to protect itself from danger, and when we experience any type of danger—from strangers to earthquakes—we are put on high alert to be careful and find safety. When our mind is fed danger from the time we wake up to the time we go to sleep, we're always on high alert. Even our dreams will be action-packed, and we'll wake up with the memory of someone chasing us, for example.

Becoming aware of our deep programming is the first step in deciding our course of action. Understanding how powerful we are as creators allows us not only to take a diet from the external news, but also to see the opportunity to invest our energy in gratitude or anything that lifts our spirits. When we surround ourselves with people who bring us down and see doom and gloom everywhere, for example, we take on their energy. This is why being aware of what and who we consume is a skill to develop as we question everything.

We can stop expecting to be led and governed by forces who don't have our best interest at heart. Just as we would not inject bleach directly into our veins, we can question the ingredients in our food supply and the quality of our water. Understanding what is natural and unnatural, what is healthy and unhealthy, will activate a feeling of power and leadership in our soul. It's almost as if our souls have been given the tools to become authentic leaders of our lives. The time for unhealthy, ego-driven leaders will end when we each take a greater role in leadership as healthy creators of our world. This can only occur when we're ready to purge our limiting beliefs and clean out the cobwebs in our minds. When we feel a strong connection to our soul and a solid grounding to the earth, healthy experiences can become real, since we're doing the work to make them happen. The key is to discover the extraordinary miracle that is you.

You might believe you don't know why you're here or have the practices you need to integrate, but what if you can sit with beliefs that are not allowing you to experience your life? Can you name them, and question each one of them until you get to the root cause? All you can do is start, and when you can ignite and trust yourself and your relationship with yourself, life will take you into the unknown. As someone who has jumped into the unknown without a parachute, I can tell you that while it wasn't easy, I would do it all again to discover what I did.

We were born for this moment in our world to say *fuck it* and question everything. Can you . . .

- Recognize the beauty within everything and everyone, including yourself?

- Focus on your opportunities? When you acknowledge and activate your opportunities, you will focus on what's possible rather than stay trapped in problems.
- Consciously choose fear or love in how you approach yourself, your community, and the world?
- Become aware of what and who is healthy and unhealthy for your body, mind, and soul?
- Constantly align your parts and integrate them to create inner balance?
- Bring your attention to your intuition?
- Take time to focus within and ignite your power source?
- Step into becoming a conscious leader and architect of humanity by living an authentic life that is healthy?

While I can't give you *your* answers or practices, I can share with you some steps I took to create healthy habits that changed my life. I relied on everything I share in the books, looking through the lens of what was healthy and unhealthy for me and what helped me fortify my immune system from toxic elements:

- Community (people, partners, and co-creators): Over time, I learned to trust myself when I felt stress around a person. I often walked away from people who wanted to fix me, save me, or take advantage of my generosity. I honed this skill over time, and I get many opportunities to experiment with it. I give people some chances, but when they squander their opportunities, I know it's now their work to do and wish them the best—not at my expense. It leaves plenty of space for heart-filled people who truly want to play and co-create with pure intention and curiosity.

- Physical health (food, diet, and exercise): I spent most of my life living in my head and ignoring my body. I was definitely out of alignment and for many years convinced myself that I came to this planet not only to create, but to cook and eat. I love food, and I love to cook. But I was very unconscious when it came to making sure that the food I consumed was healthy and natural, especially when the amount of travel I did made me rely on restaurants, airlines, and caterers to supply my nutrition, and this was insane. I learned that healthy eating increases vitality, energy, and mental clarity, and just like with the people I brought into my life, I started making healthier choices about what I consumed. It took a lot of research to learn what worked for me and what didn't. When it came to exercise, the key was how much I was moving my body and keeping it in motion. I found ways to move in the pool without injuring myself, and it's one of the things I miss most since moving. I know that where I ultimately end up will afford me a sandy beach to take long walks, and an ocean to body surf and putter around. And living in an intentional community of co-creators is something I'm curious to explore. The choices I'm planning to make take into account how I can integrate movement into my life and make sure I can maintain a healthy diet for my overall health.
- Pausing (sleep, meditation, sound healing, bodywork, rest—whatever helps us feel grounded): Moving to a rain forest changed my life, as I was a city girl most of my life. I learned that we're the ones who created property lines, as the animals showed me that everything is fair game. I saw firsthand how nature provides, and its deep divides, and I had a very different experience of and appreciation for the beauty and fierceness of nature. My sleep has always been

different, and I simply adapted to my sleep rather letting any lack of it control me. I just kept track of what fueled me and what depleted me. I don't meditate in any normal way, which shouldn't surprise anyone. I often listen to *The Icaros* beautifully created by internationally recognized opera singer, educator, sound therapist, and composer Flicka Rahn and noted multi-instrumentalist, educator, and composer/arranger Daniel Wyman. Their sound healing helps align me to the core, especially when I'm having a challenging time falling asleep. But you can choose your own way to pause to build up your immune system.

- Permission to play: A big part of shifting back into play was the willingness to let go of *should*, *could*, and *would*. It was about learning to release inner judgment that says that we must do more, be more, have more, work more, know more. I learned to be in nature as much as possible, and I spent time appreciating all its truths, really learning to relax and enjoy myself. I remembered my time as a young child running through my grandfather's almond orchard, experiencing all that surrounded us. I took myself back to being that girl who had never seen a starry sky so enchanting, or a garden so lovely. And most of all, I took myself and the world less seriously, as I relearned how to play and have fun by being in a state of appreciation and gratitude.

- Trusting the currents by letting go: By discovering my own addictions in life—from travel, to work, to being busy, to relationships—I was able to quit, or fire myself from, toxic situations. I had to rewire myself as I learned about my own prison of the mind and how to let myself out. And when I did, I slowly discovered my heartbeat and how I truly wanted to engage with life. I no longer wanted to be controlled or told how to be successful. I learned to forgive myself when I found myself in toxic situations. I asked more and more questions and also learned to love silence. Because in the silence of nature, I could hear the birds, the trees, the wind, the animals, and the ocean—and within it all, I discovered my own heartbeat and the frequency of the universe.

- Inner harmony: No matter how hard I tried, money didn't bring me happiness as I unconditioned myself from its power. I learned that accumulating more and more material possessions weighed me down. While I needed money to pay my bills, I also needed to get clear on what I really needed. As I cared less about what other people thought about me and listened more to what my soul was saying, I chased goals less and less. I realized that experiencing life was most important to me, and that it wasn't the highs or the lows that I needed to contend with, but the inner balance, harmony, and peace that I could integrate when I made healthier choices. I knew it was a bit naive, but I didn't wish for anyone else to have a war breaking out in the world as their first memory of life.

When we become aware of our mindset as a guide of our life, we become brutally aware of the failure points and weak links in our communication with ourselves and our overall health. It's about finding our strength to come back into our personal power so we can emerge as who we really are. Whatever we do, when we choose to love ourselves and not live in fear, the love will expand and the fear will no longer paralyze our energy fields, immune systems, and beliefs.

(3) There are compelling opportunities ahead when our actions match our words, thoughts, and beliefs.

We're in the midst of a global meltdown where the old paradigms are on death row, awaiting a verdict from each of us. We can choose to rage against the machine. But more of us are becoming aware that the premise of outrage, for example, is that someone holds our power. And we're giving them the power to decide our fate. While there are economic, political, educational, and many more paradigms that are no longer effective, there is another one that many of us are walking toward. This is the moment—for those of us who want to bring conscious paradigms to our world—to lead from the heart.

When it comes to breaking patterns, closing cycles, shutting doors, ending chapters—whatever words we attribute to these points in our lives—what matters most is to understand that everything has a cycle of life and death, including the systems we've created. We're increasingly questioning who has authority over our sovereignty, and we can choose to stop fighting for our lives, pointing fingers at each other, taking someone down, and suffering. We can become aware of what and who is boxing us in, and decide with compassion to consider our options.

Once we reclaim our power and make it through to the other side, there are bridges to be built to a healthy life of unity. We'll no longer need to be driven by serving our unhealthy ego from external pressures to succeed. We can have all the great ideas in the world, but if we don't act on them, they are just ideas. Author Paulo Coehlo understands us: "Before a new chapter is begun, the old one has to be finished: tell yourself that what has passed will never come back.

"Remember that there was a time when you could live without that thing or that person—nothing is irreplaceable, a habit is not a need. This may sound so obvious, it may even be difficult, but it is very important. Closing cycles. Not because of pride, incapacity or arrogance, but simply because that no longer fits your life. Shut the door, change the record, clean the house, shake off the dust. Stop being who you were, and change into who you are."

Once we can let the stories go and are able to release and detach ourselves from them, we can walk into a time of great opportunity for an individual and collective resistance of old paradigms that no longer serve us. It doesn't mean that we won't experience the desperation of the old guard doing anything in their bags of tricks to hold onto the power and maintain control. But when you're a person who feels like you don't fit in this world because you're here to create a healthier one, you'll discover your wonder in being so fucking powerful that you don't let anyone change who you are at the core.

It's time to tap into our creativity, our resilience, and our compassion—not in words, but in actions. Not by battling and fighting against what was and changing a broken system, but by creating a new design for the bridges to take us there, one step at a time. Let's find and support the pioneers who are building healthier schools, for example, outside the system. Let's thank those who brought us to this point and break away toward creating systems that keep our children healthy and provide them with what they need to live a healthy life in conjunction with nature. When we transform our problems into opportunities, we attach a vibration to what we want to create through our experiences. Every challenge or roadblock can become an opportunity to navigate and take risks in areas of our life where we may be playing it safe. Isn't it time to look inside ourselves and determine how free we are, in every area of our life, right now?

No one is going to live this life for us, and no one has the right to control us. We are the ones responsible for ourselves and are captains of our bodies, minds, and souls. Life is not always fair, and what is visible—like inequality—is often misleading until we understand the invisible pain of ourselves and each other. But regardless, we can each take responsibility for our own life. We are in charge of how we approach our challenges in life, and of determining what works and what doesn't work for us and why. What does building a meaningful life that matters mean to you?

A FEW THINGS TO CONSIDER FOR YOUR SOUL

Through the sharing of these lessons and stories, I hope you've been sparked and ignited to become aware of how you want to paint your story. Is it your time to open up healthy paths of fulfillment as you head to your future? When you choose to be an architect and an adventurer, it's about taking the road less traveled by reimagining what is possible. When you choose to pause and do your work, please consider the following:

(1) Discover the Wonder of YOU (Book 1)

Each one of us is unique and has treasures deep within. Our presence impacts those around us, often in ways that are unspoken. When a cup is empty, it cannot be used to fill another—and when a sponge is filled with water, it cannot absorb anything else. The key is to learn to take impeccable care of yourself and to trust your intuition to guide you to what's needed. Never give up, but do learn to let go of unhealthy people and situations. Allow the beauty within to find its expression, and let your inner beauty shine.

Your responsibility is to listen to what is calling you through deep self-awareness and to add your value to humanity in your own unique way. How you choose to live your life is the bottom line. You can sit and watch life pass you by, crossing items off the list, or you can jump in and become a healthy creator of your own life. It's a choice.

This adventure called life is filled with potential for you to create your own map and navigation system. The hardest work you'll ever be called to do is not at a job or on someone else's payroll, it's when you awaken to your voice and act on the treasures you uncover within. You are the main act of your life, and it's up to you to unleash your imagination to create opportunities.

(2) Trek into the Unknown as an Adventurer (Book 2)

There comes a time when it's important to close the door on the past in order to trek into the unknown. It's always helpful to be aware of the need to let go and make space for possibilities. It could be something we no longer need or use, or it could be baggage we've been carrying around for way too long. When something painful or unpleasant comes up, then it may be time to release it.

As we do, we'll feel lighter and more energized. We might also consider all that we're learning about ourselves, so we put it into action. This is a time when we can enjoy our harvest, but it's important not to be weighed down by the past and stories that no longer serve us. I often had to change direction and, on some occasions, lost my way. Despite everything, though, it was only when I paused that I began to see I was not lost at all, at least in the traditional sense. I also realized that "never burn your bridges" was a limiting belief holding me back. I simply learned which bridges should be crossed and which should be burned.

Trekking into the unknown gives us permission to experiment with being a free spirit by not being stuck in someone else's story. Our life no longer depends on anyone else's survival, because we're more powerful than we ever could have imagined when we know our hearts and minds. We're deeply connected to nature as a curious and courageous adventurer—a dreamer, an architect, and a creator of a healthy life. We know there's only one success: living our lives in our own ways. Our self-love shines on the life and communities we build, and we know a healthy world is possible.

(3) Trust Your Heart and Be Health-Conscious (Book 3)

Once we realize there's always a way—whether we like it or not—so much can shift. Artist and spiritual teacher Florence Scovel Shinn said, "Intuition is a spiritual faculty and does not explain, but simply points the way." When we're not sure of the way forward or the answer to a particular question, the path lies in being still and hearing our inner voice. This can be felt as an inner knowing or a feeling—or we might have a profound dream or a sign from the Universe. These are all valid ways of tuning in to the wise part of us that is all-knowing, so we have no need to feel powerless. We might have to alter our definition of power from being in charge to surrendering and trusting the currents.

Antoine de Saint-Exupéry, in *The Little Prince*, reminds us that "it is only with the heart that one can see rightly; what is essential is invisible to the eye." Simply learn to listen to your gut. Feel free to ask it questions, but also respect it by fully being in tune with what it is whispering to you. Once the whispers become clearer, you can listen to it as quietly or loudly as you prefer. And if something is stopping you, invest the energy in understanding where fear or worry stem from so you can assess the root cause and then listen some more. Your schooling may have taught you to think logically, but your heart never lies.

A JOURNEY LIKE NO OTHER

An experienced ship captain can skirt some storms that may trap less experienced navigators. But even the most experienced cannot avoid every storm. Some storms in life will take us off course. When it comes to weathering a storm on a ship, we would prefer having a skilled captain at the helm. But in life, we become aware that knowing how to navigate to stay on course for a fixed destination may not be our preferred course of action.

When we don't currently live a life we like, then we have an opportunity to understand why we're here on this planet. Some of us came here to raise children, and others came here to farm. Some of us came to imagine, and others came to create. When we stop the madness of comparing how much we've achieved, we can start our journey of self-awareness and discovery. It doesn't matter how old you are—you can start at eighty-seven or eleven. Everyone has the same opportunity to become really present in daily life. As we do, we'll discover joy in the details.

We are being called to pause and experience our bodies in a holistic way. We've been conditioned that if we stop and rest, we're lazy or unproductive. We've learned that we have been allocated to rest and find joy when we're on vacation or when we finally get to retire from a life of work. We rush to the gym, often forgetting that although our bodies need movement and motion, creating stress around making it to our workout or meditation class doesn't help the body.

Wisdom lies in knowing that we are more than our bodies and becoming aware of our divine essence. This means that we can find natural ways of relating to the physical world around us. To better understand this, visualize what it might be like to live a harmonious life. See yourself as a truly healthy person, or visualize your idea of the ultimate healthy world. Take as much time as you need. Once you've captured the images, make a list of or draw whatever you saw.

We face a choice in every moment to touch lives in ways that encourage humility, beauty, and harmony, or in ways that spread division, distrust, and pain. From the perspective of our soul, a healthy life is not measured in money, power, or social status. We're being asked to connect with ourselves and allow our curiosity and imagination to expand into uncharted territories. It requires compassion, and curiosity to find our own authenticity and vulnerability. It is part of being human and being connected to universal, natural laws. It allows us to discover our own power and awe, while respecting that we are each on our own journey, going at our own pace.

I hope you discover whatever is calling you. We're here to create and live with deep meaning—and to usher in a healthy world it's going to take a great deal of individual and collective work of reimagining how to connect with ourselves and jump off the pages of how we were instructed to live our life. Please ask yourself, "Might it be time for me to listen to the whispers of my soul?"

When we question, we find the courage to test the answers that start showing up in our life. Many of us spend years questioning, cultivating our vision, and running down rabbit holes before becoming aware of what's healthy and unhealthy for us. These books can become trusted resources for you to come back to again and again, when you need to trek into an expedition that's calling you. Each time you open your own book, you can find, somewhere in the pages, what you need most, wherever you are on your journey. The book chose us, at this moment. Please share it with anyone who can benefit from experiencing it so healthy dialogue can emerge about what matters most to you.

When we consume unconsciously—whether it's the news twenty-four hours a day or beliefs that deplete us—we become fearful and nervous and fall into many rabbit holes. The opportunity each one of us is facing, when we're ready, is to really look at ourselves, reimagine what's possible, ground ourselves, and take impeccable care of our bodies, our minds, our souls, and each other. It's time to see and act holistically and with unity, not conformity or uniformity, understanding how everything in the universe is connected by design. Remember that when we're all sad and fearful, this energy storms and vibrates through us and many storms appear in our lives and our world. There's strength in uncovering pure joy and rewiring our energy source to have more balance. Every person who is ready to journey into the unknown is being asked to face our fears and limiting beliefs. Allow yourself to emerge with a vision and a remembrance of why you are here. What do you want to build and create? And don't forget to sing, dance, run, scream, let go, and cleanse, so you can create through alchemy and pure authentic love of yourself and the planet.

When one stage of our journey ends, another begins. See you soon for our continuing journey in *F*ck the Bucket List for the Adventurer: Trekking into the Unknown.*

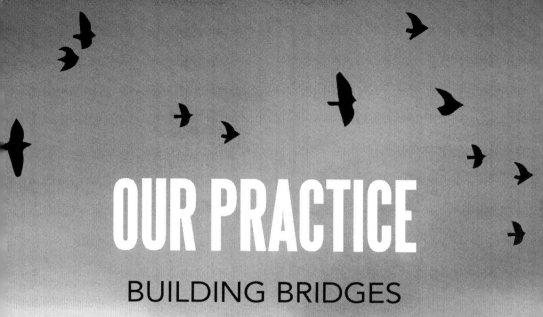

OUR PRACTICE
BUILDING BRIDGES

*

EPILOGUE

Human history, as recorded in our history books, calls for the death of one leader, one regime, one paradigm to usher in a better one. Much energy goes into discrediting the evils of one simply by replacing it with another. And yet, despite all the revolutions, uprisings, genocides, and efforts to save the world, our history simply repeats itself over and over.

We could be in an unhealthy relationship with a partner or a boss, and dream of a new person who will better appreciate us—but we might just keep bringing the same person, with a different face and body, into our lives. Just changing the deck chairs on a sinking ship is not enough. It's time to go deeper in understanding the root causes of our situations, and get back in harmony with nature's intelligence and our own power sources.

The bridge, like the rainbow, is a symbol of passage to another level of existence—connecting one to another. In ancient cultures, the construction of bridges was considered sacred and would be accompanied by rituals to secure passage. Bridges are like stories. When we analyze the voices in our mind and see the opportunity to unite ourselves, we can start building the bridges between where we are and where we're guided to exist. Stories also serve as bridges between cultures with their power to bring people together by connecting hearts, imagination, and ability to construct.

Today, many of our paradigms are collapsing, and that is our opportunity to build healthy bridges—starting with ourselves. It's about building a connection, a bridge, to ourselves, each other, and the planet. As long as we can construct our stories from our hearts, nothing is lost. We're always transforming. The house or structure you live in may have wood floors or beams that were once trees in the forest. The necklace or shirt you're wearing may be organic or modified with synthetics. Everything starts with nature, and we transform it through our imagination and curiosity. We build physical bridges from material and invisible bridges with our beliefs. Sometimes we believe we're stuck and there's nowhere to go, but that is when we upgrade our own operating systems to take us on a journey of discovery, accepting that there's no final destination and there's always a way when we flow with life.

When we take a journey into the mind of anyone who we believe has it all, we feel that we'll experience the perfect life, the life most people dream of achieving. But what we'll most likely experience is that their life is so perfect that to them, it has lost some of its meaning. This person may be a stay-at-home dad happily married to a wealthy investor who loves him very much. The couple has wonderful twin girls, the perfect home, and every luxury money can buy.

In living within society's demands and the expectations created for them, the dad might have constantly been seeking love in an effort not to disappoint anyone. Too often, he forgets that he is someone.

Life offers us thousands of opportunities for learning. One day at the park, the dad overhears a conversation in which one woman tells another that all she wants is to live an unpredictable life rather than a happy one, as there's mystery in being passionate about life and not knowing what might happen next. The conversation turns this man's life upside down, and he starts feeling an urge to question everything, especially what happens when life is exactly the way he envisioned it and his life has become full of responsibilities. Battling with these questions, his perfect world brings him on a journey he never imagined, with bridges that he chose to build to the world of his deepest dreams with his family. It was always under his nose; he just had to unlock his heart.

Knowing ourselves not only involves being aware of what comforts us but also being aware of our shadows. This requires a lot of courage. Not everyone is brave enough to face themselves. This is why many choose to distract ourselves through illusions. Aldous Huxley reminds us, "There is only one corner of the universe you can be certain of improving, and that's your own self." The important thing isn't what happens to you, but how you face it. Your attitude and mindset help build the bridges needed to trek into the unknown in high awareness of what's possible.

And once again, the wisdom of our elders. In *The Republic,* Plato reminds us that "the beginning is the most important part of the work." Are you ready to stand strong in your integrity, your power, and your mastery? Now is the time not only to make your choices about what's healthy and toxic but to begin channeling your energy. Choose wisely, for your choices will affect you and future generations for decades to come.

TO BE CONTINUED . . .

F*ck the Bucket List for the Adventurer:
Trekking into the Unknown

F*ck the Bucket List for the Health-Conscious:
Trusting Your Heart

You're invited to visit
<u>ayeletbaron.com</u>
and download
the first expedition of
book two in the series...

F*ck the Bucket List
for the Adventurer:
Trekking into the Unknown

Made in United States
Orlando, FL
01 November 2022

24114059R00137